THOMAS JEFFERSON

&

EDUCATION

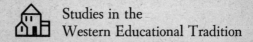 Studies in the
Western Educational Tradition

Consulting Editor

PAUL NASH • *Boston University*

THOMAS JEFFERSON & EDUCATION

Robert D. Heslep

• *University of Georgia* •

RANDOM HOUSE • NEW YORK

TO JOELYN MILLER HESLEP

PERMISSIONS ACKNOWLEDGMENTS

To The University of North Carolina Press for permission to quote material from *The Adams–Jefferson Letters*, edited by L. J. Cappon.

To The Johns Hopkins University Press for permission to quote from *The Commonplace Book of Thomas Jefferson: A Repertory of His Ideas on Government*, edited by Gilbert Chinard.

To the editors of *Educational Theory* for permission to reprint material from Robert D. Heslep, "Thomas Jefferson's Major Philosophical Principles," Vol. XVI, No. 2, April 1966, 152–161.

To The Princeton University Press for permission to use material from *The Papers of Thomas Jefferson*, edited by Julian P. Boyd *et al.*, Vol. I, 1760–1776 (1950) and Vol. II, 1777–1779 (1950). Copyright, 1950, by Princeton University Press; London: Geoffrey Cumberlege, Oxford University Press.

Contents

THOMAS
JEFFERSON
&
EDUCATION

· I ·
Introduction

During his lifetime Thomas Jefferson was regarded as a significant figure in numerous areas of thought and action. He was esteemed for his talent and accomplishments in such fields as natural science, education, agriculture, architecture, and technology as well as politics. For a number of decades after his death, however, there was a remarkable narrowing of cognizance of his far-ranging genius. He came to be remembered, by the scholarly as well as the popular mind, predominantly for his contributions to the field of politics. Happily, the present century has, to an important extent, restored the balance; for within the past fifty years Jefferson has again come to be considered, at least by the scholarly mind, as a significant person in many fields of theoretical and practical concern. A factor contributing to this revived appreciation of his diverse talents and achievements has been the research undertaken during this century to assemble and edit his writings. By the turn of the century there had been several attempts to publish comprehensive editions of Jefferson's papers.[1] Unfortunately, all these editions omitted, individually and collectively, many of his writings; and some of the collections were unsatisfactorily edited. It was not until the second quarter of this century that the whole of his extant works,[2] in accordance with the rigor of modern scholarship, was brought to press.

One of the areas of Jefferson's thought which has come to be of special interest in this generation is that of education. Some scholars now consider his basic ideas on education worthy of serious examination.[3] He is regarded by numerous contemporary historians of education as having formulated educational policies, programs, and plans of historical moment.[4] And his educational proposals are held by a number of critics to be useful for identifying and settling many of today's educational problems.[5] As a result, a notable amount of literature devoted to Jefferson's connection with education has appeared recently. Jefferson's role as an educational leader in the United States, the fact that he lived during a revolutionary period of Western society, and his strong intellectual interests make the topic of his contributions to Western education appear promising. Inevitably, perhaps, investigations into the topic have been mixed in quality, ranging from superficial to profound. Yet, regardless of their individual merits and defects, they have generally discounted an important feature. In defining Jefferson's contributions to Western education, scholars have largely regarded his educational proposals as the main source of his contributions. And, in making this assumption, they appear to have been on fairly solid ground. The difficulty is that they have usually given only scant attention to the relationship between Jefferson's educational proposals and the principles on which they rest. More specifically, they have not seriously considered what significance the principles have for the proposals as contributions to Western education. As a consequence, scholars have ignored some vital points. It seems pertinent, therefore, to direct an inquiry at this relationship.

Neither Jefferson's educational proposals nor the principles on which they rest were formulated or conceived in a historical vacuum; rather, they were shaped, to an important degree, by the economic, political, social, and cultural factors of the milieu in which Jefferson lived. By examining the relation of the proposals and principles to these factors, one will be in a position to enhance his comprehension of the former. A way to investigate this relationship is, first, to consider what the elements of Jefferson's historical situation were and, second, to determine the influence of these factors upon the development of his philosophical ideas and educational proposals.

Consequently, the present essay will follow a roundabout route in arriving at an understanding of Jefferson's contributions to Western education insofar as they relate to his philosophical principles. In reaching that understanding, the essay includes an exploration of the economic, political, social, and cultural forces of Jefferson's milieu; a consideration of the influence of these forces upon the development of his philosophical ideas and educational proposals; an examination of his philosophical ideas; and a study of his theoretical and practical educational proposals.

· NOTES ·

1. See *Memoir, Correspondence, and Miscellanies, from the Papers of Thomas Jefferson*, Thomas Jefferson Randolph (ed.), 2nd ed., 4 vols. (Boston: Gray & Bowen, 1830). *The Writings of Thomas Jefferson*, Henry A. Washington (ed.), 9 vols. (Washington, D.C.: Taylor & Maury, 1853–1854). *The Writings of Thomas Jefferson*, "Memorial Edition," A. A. Lipscomb and A. E. Bergh (eds.), 20 vols. (Washington, D.C.: Thomas Jefferson Memorial Association, 1903–1904). *The Works of Thomas Jefferson*, "Federal Edition," P. L. Ford (ed.), 12 vols. (New York: Putnam, 1904–1905).

2. See *The Commonplace Book of Thomas Jefferson: A Repertory of His Ideals on Government*, with an Introduction and notes by Gilbert Chinard (Baltimore: The Johns Hopkins University Press, 1926). *The Literary Bible of Thomas Jefferson: His Commonplace Book of Philosophers and Poets*, with an Introduction by Gilbert Chinard (Baltimore: The Johns Hopkins University Press, 1928). *Thomas Jefferson's Garden Book, 1766–1824*, annotated by E. M. Betts (Philadelphia: The American Philosophical Society, 1944). *The Adams-Jefferson Letters*, L. J. Cappon (ed.), 2 vols. (Chapel Hill: The University of North Carolina Press, 1959). *The Papers of Thomas Jefferson*, Julian P. Boyd *et al.* (eds.), 17 vols. published, 50 vols. projected (Princeton, N.J.: Princeton University Press, 1950 et seq.).

3. Cf. Gordon C. Lee, "Learning and Liberty: The Jeffer-

sonian Tradition in Education," in Gordon C. Lee (ed.), *Crusade Against Ignorance: Thomas Jefferson On Education* (New York: Bureau of Publications of Teachers College, Columbia University, 1962).

4. Cf. John S. Brubacher, *A History of the Problems of Education* (New York: McGraw-Hill, 1947), *ad passim*. Mehdi Nakosteen, *The History and Philosophy of Education* (New York: The Ronald Press, 1965), pp. 451 ff. Robert Ulich, *History of Educational Thought* (New York: American Book, 1950), pp. 242–257.

5. The wide variety of educational problems on which Jefferson has been consulted is suggested by the following titles: James B. Conant, "Education for a Classless Society; the Jeffersonian Tradition," *Atlantic Monthly*, CLXV (May 1940), 593–602. S. E. Morison, "Is Liberal Education Democratic: What Jefferson Advocated," *Hispania*, XXVII (February 1944), 78. N. Sand, "Classics in Jefferson's Theory of Education," *Classics Journal*, XL (November 1944), 92–98. G. E. Baker, "Thomas Jefferson on Academic Freedom," *American Association of University Professors Bulletin*, XXXIX (September 1953), 377–387. Robert M. Healey, *Jefferson on Religion in Public Education* (New Haven, Conn.: Yale University Press, 1962).

· II ·
Jefferson's
Historical
Milieu

Thomas Jefferson was born in Virginia on April 13, 1743. Some of the factors that helped to shape his educational thought existed in Virginia at the time of his birth, and many of those that appeared later can best be comprehended if they are related to mid-eighteenth-century Virginia. Before examining Jefferson's life with a view to specifying the factors contributing to his thinking on education, one will do well to take a look at his native Virginia. A helpful way to do this is to consider its major aspects as a society organized, for the most part, around a landed aristocracy.

I

Prior to the American Revolution, Virginia was economically enmeshed in the English mercantile system. Like England's other American colonies, Virginia was regarded by both Crown and Parliament as a major source of wealth for the mother country and, as a supplier of goods, was expected to send surplus crops, manufactures, and extractive products primarily to England. For the benefit of the mother country's shipbuilders and owners, the colony was expected to export its goods on English bottoms. And, as a consumer of the mother country's surplus products, it was expected to purchase the bulk of its imports from England. Virginia, although subservient in this system, had nevertheless developed a fairly complex internal economic structure.

The heart of Virginia's prerevolutionary economy was its plantation, or farm, system. At the beginning of the eighteenth century, the colony's plantations, numbering in the thousands, were located almost entirely on the coastal plain, known as the tidewater area and bounded on the west by the river fall line. Only a small number of the plantations were as large as several thousand acres; and very few of them were larger than 5,000 acres. Perhaps as many as 90 percent of the planters had holdings ranging between 50 and 500 acres.[1] By 1730, because of the scarcity of land in the tidewater region, the spreading exhaustion of tidewater land by tobacco farming, and the British government's newly lenient measures for the purchase and settlement of Virginia's frontier lands, there was a move to buy and settle the piedmont and valley lands, the former lying between the fall line and the Blue Ridge Mountains and the latter lying between the Blue Ridge and the Allegheny Mountains.[2] Because the terms of purchase and settlement were liberal, the acquisition of huge tracts for speculation was encouraged, while the founding of many large plantations ranging from several thousand to tens of thousands of acres was also fostered. Indeed, the pioneer leaders of Virginia's westerward expansion were those who bought such plantations—planters, lawyers, merchants, ministers, and physicians from the tidewater area. Because of the need for transportation to and from the coast, the most desirable of the new plantation sites were in the piedmont region along the Potomac, Rappahannock, James, and other rivers giving access to the coast. It was on these sites that the large plantations were usually located. The speculators in the frontier lands often subdivided their tracts into small farms for sale or rent, and the large plantation owners frequently rented small parts of their lands to tenants. By 1763 the western lands were all settled thickly enough to be organized into counties. By inheritance and fortunate marriages, planters both east and west of the fall line were able to add to their holdings; and, through laws favoring primogeniture and entailment, they were able to keep their estates intact.

The planters found tobacco, their major cash crop, troublesome. The more desirable varieties of tobacco (Orinoco and Sweet Scented) were rather difficult to cultivate, and the farming of the crop rapidly wore out the land. Overproduction kept the price of tobacco low (often, no more than a penny per pound). And shipping costs, warehouse and brokerage fees, and English import duties severely limited the planter's profits from the crop. In fact, some of the planters who settled west of the fall line found that their lands were not satisfactory for tobacco. Toward the middle of the eighteenth century, the planters endeavored to improve their lot through diversification. They started growing crops other than tobacco, such as wheat, corn, and flax; and they began plantation manu-

factures, such as milling, weaving, beef and pork pack-
ing, and tanning. Although such diversifications were
fairly widespread, they generally remained secondary
sources of income for the planters. In 1755, as Governor
Dinwiddie reported to the Board of Trade and Plantations
in England, Virginia exported 200,000 bushels of corn
(12,500 pounds sterling) but the colony also was ap-
proaching by this time an annual tobacco export average
of 50,000 hogsheads (500,000 pounds sterling).[3]

At the beginning of the eighteenth century, when virtually all the plantations were situated in the tidewater
region, many of the planters, the large bulk of whom were
yeomen, performed their own labor; and numerous of
them had one or two field hands. Only a comparative few
possessed a large group of workers, say, ten or more. Of
the people who labored for the planters at this time about
4,000 were bond servants and about 6,000 were slaves.[4]
As the century unfolded, the growth of plantations in size
and number made great numbers of field hands necessary.
Many planters relied increasingly on slave trade to provide
them with laborers, because the supply of bond servants
did not increase appreciably and it was thought that slaves
would be cheaper to maintain than bond servants. In
1708 there were, perhaps, 12,000 slaves in Virginia; in
1730, there were approximately 30,000; and in 1763, according to Governor Fauquier's report to the Board of
Trade and Plantations, there were about 120,000—close to
the total number of white people in the colony at the
time. Although the wealthy planters owned large gangs of
slaves, small planters, who typically had only a few slaves,
possessed collectively the majority of the slaves. At the
outbreak of the American Revolution, Virginia's non-slave-

holding planters lived mostly in the valley and constituted the bulk of that region's population.

In the larger towns as well as on the greater plantations of colonial Virginia, manufacturing was being done by competent craftsmen, including millers, brewers, weavers, butchers, tanners, shoemakers, blacksmiths, sawyers, brickmakers, and shipwrights. The artisans on plantations were usually slaves, whereas those in the towns were freemen. A variety of the products—notably, beef, pork, flour, staves, plank, shingles, tar, and turpentine—were exported along with the tobacco and cereal crops. By way of imports Virginia received slaves, woolen and linen goods, furniture, stockings, silks, shoes, ornaments, wine, rum, strong beer, sugar, salt, and other commodities. Frequently, the planters purchased imported goods directly from foreign merchants; but they also bought them from the Virginia merchants, who lived mainly in the coastal towns. Because the planters depended for the bulk of their cash upon seasonal crops, they usually made their purchases on credit; and, because they had no way of forecasting their crop income accurately, they were often in debt. At the outbreak of the revolution, Virginia owed English merchants $10 million. Both the interior and the coastal towns had shopkeepers, and from time to time peddlers ventured into the western counties.

During the American Revolution Virginia's economy suffered.[5] Because the export trade with England was disrupted, the price of grains fell sharply; and that of certain necessities (for example, salt, which was needed in the curing of meats) rose steeply. In the tidewater and piedmont regions, British forces destroyed some planters' crops and residences, carried off several hundred slaves, and burned the town of Norfolk. Supplies had to be furnished by the countryside for the care of prisoners as well as revolutionary troops, but the state government frequently failed to provide compensation for property conscripted from planters. Taxes were higher than they had been before the war. In the decade following the battle at Yorktown, the tidewater and piedmont areas made a fair recovery—at least, they enjoyed a good tobacco market when trade was resumed with England and its possessions.[6] The planters in the valley region, however, continued to suffer because they had poor transportation to and from coastal port towns and interstate duties were levied on the goods that they sent through Pennsylvania and Maryland. Many of the non-slave-holding planters tried to solve their plight by moving into the cheap and recently opened trans-Allegheny lands, where they could ship their products by river to New Orleans. Before leaving Virginia, they often sold their small holdings to slave-owning planters, thereby helping to make possible the spread and engrossment of slave-worked plantations. By the turn of the century, conditions were somewhat improved: the piedmont and valley regions were selling huge quantities of wheat to Europe, the tidewater and piedmont areas had greatly expanded their lumber industry, cotton was rivaling tobacco as an export staple, and the city of Richmond was exporting hundreds of shiploads of coal yearly to New York and Philadelphia.

II

Being a royal colony (one that was a personal possession of the king), prerevolutionary Virginia was under direct monarchical rule, but it was not necessarily subject, for that reason, to tyranny. It was assumed in both England and Virginia that the citizens of the colony should enjoy the same liberties, franchises, and immunities that they should enjoy if they were born and resided in England. And this meant, in part, that they ought to have a definite amount of self-government. The famous charges of tyranny against the monarchy were not made until the reign of George III, when Virginians thought that their rights were being seriously violated.

As the ruler of Virginia, the king was holder of its lands; he received revenues through the sale of the lands and the quitrents placed upon all those sold. He was not interested, however, in ruling the colony merely to obtain personal wealth but governed it also with a view to benefitting England commercially and otherwise. To help formulate and execute policies for Virginia and the other royal colonies, the monarch appointed a council resident in England and, in addition, governors to reside in the colonies. In the eighteenth century the council was known as the Board of Trade and Plantations.

The governor of the colony, whose seat of government was Williamsburg, possessed strong and varied powers, legislative and judicial as well as executive.[7] He appointed and, when necessary, suspended the members of his advisory council. He alone had the power to convoke, prorogue, and dissolve the colony's legislative body, the General Assembly. As a member of the assembly he could stop the passage of any act by withholding his assent, and as an executive he could veto any act passed by the assembly (but even an act with his approval was subject to the king's veto). He sat as the head of the General Court (which was the colony's main court) and commissioned judges and other officials of the colony's judicial administration. He alone had the authority to levy, arm, and muster the militia. And among other duties, he granted, with his council's consent, all patents to the colony's public lands. By way of remuneration the governor was provided with a handsome salary, a mansion in Williamsburg, occasional gifts from his council and the House of Burgesses, and tributes, at times, from Indians. During the eighteenth century, at least until the critical years preceding the revolution, Virginia's governors were generally competent and beneficent. At times in this period the governors were, strictly speaking, lieutenant governors who carried on the administration while the actual governors stayed in England and enjoyed their salaries as political favors.

The governor's advisory council, by royal instruction, consisted of Virginians with both property and ability.[8] As citizens of the colony, they were acquainted with its particular circumstances. Being able, they helped to ensure (with such exceptions as shall be indicated shortly) the proper rule of the colony; and, having wealth, they commanded public respect and were prepared to cover the deficits in their official accounts. A majority of the members came from tidewater planter families, and a few were trained in law. Although the members of the council were mainly advisors to the governor, they had numerous other duties. They constituted the upper chamber of the General Assembly, sat with the governor on the General Court, acted as escheators, collected the colony's export duties on tobacco and other goods, and served as colonels in the militia. The president of the council acted in lieu of the governor whenever he was absent from the colony, and other members served as colonial secretary and colonial auditor. For serving as advisors, legislators, and judges, the council members received only a modest salary; but they found their other duties to be rather lucrative. As export duty collectors, they were granted a percentage of their collections, which were considerable; and, in violation of the law, they were inclined to be lenient in collecting the taxes on their own exports. By virtue of their access to land records, they were in a position to win contracts from the crown to collect, for a fee, the royal quitrents that were in arrears. And as escheators they did receive some earnings. In brief, the council enabled its wealthy members to become even richer; and because of this comfortable arrangement, the members were not easily tempted to risk suspension by determinedly supporting views of the colonists which opposed the governor's desires.

Colonial Virginia's chief institution of self-government was the lower chamber of the General Assembly, the House of Burgesses.[9] Unlike the members of the governor's advisory council, those of the House of Burgesses were not appointed by any royal agent, but were elected by a popular ballot. And unlike the governor or his advisors, the Burgesses alone, by tradition, possessed the authority to initiate legislation concerning the internal affairs of the colony, for example, domestic taxes, education, the construction of roads, and the navigability of rivers. Although prerevolutionary Virginia's franchise had a property qualification, it was not seriously limiting for that reason. Any adult white male could vote if he owned (1) 100 acres of land, (2) 25 acres with a house and a plantation, or (3) a house and a lot in a town. And, because the price of land stayed rather low, the property qualification did not prevent very many adult white males from voting. Even though the majority of voters were common people, they usually elected their representatives to the House of Burgesses from the foremost citizens of the colony. On the other hand, the Burgesses were often solicitous to the interests of their respective constituencies. Each county, the large towns, and the College of William and Mary were represented in the House of Burgesses. Because the tidewater district had more counties and large towns than the piedmont or valley region, it had more representatives than the other districts. Actually, it had more representatives per 1,000 white adult males—a fact that is explainable by the westward shift of prerevolutionary Virginia's white population.

Within the two decades preceding the American Revolution, there were a number of notable political issues in Virginia, some of which arose from the colony's sectional differences. The planters of Virginia's interior sought public funds for improved river and road transportation from their lands to the coast, but they were often opposed by the tidewater and some of the piedmont planters. Of those planters living in the valley region, most had small holdings and belonged to Baptist, Presbyterian, and other sects dissenting from the Anglican Church, which was strong in the piedmont and tidewater areas and which, being England's national church, was supported in Virginia by public revenue. These small planters distrusted the large tidewater and piedmont planters, especially the governor's advisory council, and objected to being compelled to help support the Anglican Church. There was also in the western half of the colony a noticeable opposition to slavery, which came mainly, but not exclusively, from the non-slave-holding planters, who feared the competition of slave labor and who, as in the case of those who were Quakers and Baptists, frequently had religious scruples about the institution.

Other political issues involved relations between England and Virginia. The pistole fee, which, by the governor's order, had to be paid for the use of his seal on all land patents, forced the question of whether or not the governor or any other royal agent had the authority to impose an internal tax upon the colonials. The Two Penny Act, which was passed by the General Assembly to fix the Anglican clergy's salary by having it paid in money rather than tobacco (but which was disallowed by the Crown), led to discussions of the British constitution and self-government. And the celebrated Stamp Act and Townshend duties compelled the General Assembly to re-examine Virginia's constitutional relations with England. It was from the debates of this second group of issues that there emerged the men who were to lead the colonies during the American Revolution.

Shortly after the revolution began, the interim government of the newly independent Virginia drew up a constitution for the state. In one respect, the instrument attempted to rectify unsatisfactory features of the colonial government and reflected definite democratic tendencies. More specifically, it included a fairly strong bill of rights and proposed a government with much of its power vested in a popular legislature. The legislature consisted of a

House of Delegates and a Senate, with the members of each popularly elected. The governor was elected by the legislators and was further restrained by an executive council appointed by them. Also, the higher members of the judiciary were made elective by the legislature. Nevertheless, the constitution did not overcome all old problems nor did it contain wholly democratic principles. Most significantly, it permitted the legislative body to be malapportioned. Each county in the state was allowed two members in the House of Delegates; each of the large towns was permitted three representatives; and each senatorial district was allowed one senator. Because the tidewater region contained more counties, large towns, and senatorial districts than either the piedmont or the valley area, it was in a position to influence considerably, if not dominate, the government. The tidewater area had, however, far fewer enfranchised people per representative than either of the other regions. By 1790 the tidewater region had one representative in the House of Delegates for every 596 white males sixteen years old or over, the valley region had one representative for every 1408 such males, and the piedmont district had one representative for every 953.[10]

Because of the heady atmosphere of the revolution, the legislature came under a democratic influence long enough to pass measures aimed at breaking the aristocratic power of the large planters: It abolished primogeniture, entailment, and the slave trade. Subsequently, however, the large planters of the tidewater and, in part, the piedmont regions regained their control and stopped further radical economic reforms; and they prevented a rewriting of the constitution when it was advocated by representatives from the western part of the state. Several years after

the economic reforms were enacted, the privileged position of the Episcopalian (formerly Anglican) Church in
Virginia was abolished; but most of the other attempts at
democratic social reform, for example, the establishment
of a general system of education, were futile. Virginia,
fearing a loss of sovereignty if it submitted to a strong
central national government, ratified the American constitution with some reluctance; and during the first decade of
the new national government the state led the opposition
against federal administration measures that appeared to
favor Northern interests at the expense of Southern ones.

III

In considering the social aspect of colonial Virginia, one
cannot ignore the royal governor, the colony's most prominent social person. Often, he came from a highly important English family; and, even if he did not, as in the case
of some of the lieutenant governors, he held at least a
notable position in English society. Along with his English social standing, his education, wealth, and authority
commanded the respect, if not admiration, of virtually all
members of the colony. Nevertheless, a more important
element of colonial Virginia's society was its class structure.[11]

The highest ranking social class was the planter aristocracy. Within this class there were three groups:
wealthy planters who belonged to long-established families, planters who came from prominent families but who
were not especially wealthy, and planters who had great
wealth but who did not belong to important families. The
concern with family prestige led a number of the aristo-

cratic planters to seek out the heraldry that might have belonged to their English ancestors. Because the rich planter aristocrats could afford overseers to supervise the work on their holdings and domestic servants to care for their large and often splendid plantation residences, they enjoyed the advantages of a leisurely life. They indulged in a variety of amusements and pastimes, such as elegant dinners, musical soirées, plays, horse races, and fox hunts. To display their wealth and position, they wore wigs, silks, and silver buckles, purchased imported furniture, employed fine liveries, and had their portraits painted. They assured themselves, however, of a substantial education: the sons usually attended college, and the daughters normally received a young lady's finishing education. In addition, the planter aristocrats enjoyed certain privileges: when, for example, one of them was guilty of a crime normally punished by the lash, he was likely to receive nothing more than a fine payable in tobacco.

What may be viewed as the next highest class in pre-revolutionary Virginia consisted of a variety of people: Anglican ministers, merchants, smaller but substantial planters, and successful shopkeepers. Although the members of this class lived in comparative modesty, they had comfortable homes and a few servants, bond or slave. Moreover, they normally secured for their sons at least a secondary schooling and for their daughters a primary one. Occasionally individuals of this class became, through fortunate investments, members of the planter aristocracy. The third class contained the artisans and poorer shopkeepers, whose incomes and dwellings were very small and whose sons usually received nothing more than a primary schooling and an apprenticeship. The next class, living mostly in the western half of the colony, were the poor planters, many of whom were Scotch-Irish and German immigrants. Frequently they belonged to non-Anglican religious groups; they usually lived in crude cabins, sometimes with nothing upon which to sleep but bunks or floors; and they could afford no servants. It was normal for their children to be illiterate. The bond servants, upon completion of their respective periods of servitude, sometimes became small planters or undertook some trade or business. The slaves, of course, had no better life than that which their masters allowed, and it was of a mean sort for the field hands. The few free Negroes in the colony were subject to segregation, and the Indians were confined to reservations. Although there was a generally stable family life among the white people in the colony, there was a noticeable number of white pauper children —orphans and neglected children with no means of support. Their care was the responsibility of local communities.

The attempts at democratic reform that succeeded in Virginia during and following the American Revolution —the abolition of primogeniture, entailment, and the slave trade—affected the state's social order in only minor ways. There was no longer a royal governor to be the leading social figure, but the planter aristocracy remained the dominant class. The wealthy planters employed their considerable influence in the malapportioned legislature to look after their economic and social interests; at the same time they failed to use their power to improve the lot of the lower classes. Even though the absence of laws favoring primogeniture and entailment led to the dismemberment of a few estates, it did not prevent the wealthy planters from engrossing themselves by buying up the holdings of the small planters who left Virginia to cross the Allegheny Mountains. The proscription of the slave trade did not stop the increase of the slave population through reproduction and the institution of a domestic slave market. The restoration of trade with England and the development of industries (for example, coal and lumber) enabled merchants and businessmen to increase their wealth and maintain the social prestige that they had had prior to the revolution.

IV

Eighteenth-century colonial Virginia did not have a rich culture. Because the colony was comparatively new, pre-occupied with agriculture, and accustomed to the fine arts and scholarship of the Old World, it did not produce poets, artists, composers, or scholars. Moreover, it had only one or two bookstores and only one newspaper, the Virginia *Gazette* (published in Williamsburg). Even so, it had a culture that was notable in at least two respects, intellectual life and formal education. The planter aristocracy enjoyed these more than any of the other classes.

Although Virginia's aristocrats were disposed to regard horse racing, cock fighting, fox hunting, and card playing as some of their favorite amusements, they also found chamber music a delightful pastime and sought entertainment at Williamsburg's repertory theater, which staged plays by Shakespeare, Congreve, Garrick, and others. They displayed a fair taste in architecture and gardening. Moreover, they valued, for its own sake and for its usefulness, the cultivation of their minds. Although they did not stand at the middle of the eighteenth-century Enlightenment, they were within its periphery.[12]

Toward the close of the seventeenth century, there were, perhaps, only 20,000 books in Virginia. Practically all of them were in private libraries, which were owned mostly by aristocratic planters and only a few of which exceeded several hundred titles. Many of the small planters were illiterate and did not own even a Bible. At the approach of the American Revolution, the large majority of the books in the colony were still in the libraries of aristocratic planters; but the number of the books had greatly increased. William Byrd II possessed about 4,000 volumes; Robert Carter III, around 1,500; John Mercer, about 1,500; and George Washington, approximately 900. Typically, the largest collection in an aristocratic planter's library consisted of Latin and Greek classics, including tomes by Homer, Plutarch, Ovid, and Cicero. Seemingly, these were read to gain instruction as well as pleasure. The next largest group, reflecting the planter's concern with politics and legal problems, was made up of works of law, some being theoretical but most being practical treatises. The remainder of the library contained an assortment of volumes in modern history, philosophy, geography, science, religion, and literature and in such other areas as surveying, gardening, and medicine. Although the Virginia aristocrats were especially fond of classical authors, they were also quite interested in modern English writers. They read Shakespeare, Bacon, Milton, Bunyan, Pope, Locke, Shaftesbury, Kames, Swift, Fielding, and others but seemed to show little enthusiasm for continental authors, who were represented in the libraries by only a few names, most notably, Montesquieu.

It seems doubtless that this penchant for serious and extensive reading contributed to the competence and ingenuity which the aristocratic planters displayed in their dealings with Virginia's political affairs.

But there was more to colonial Virginia's intellectual life than private libraries. There was also an active (although modest) interest in science. Of those who engaged in scientific pursuits some were planters and ministers, but others were distinct naturalists. None, however, contributed anything directly to the theoretical development of science. By and large, they confined themselves to discovering facts about Virginia's natural environment, its plants, animals, and minerals. Some of their findings were published by England's Royal Society. Although the planters were not scientific farmers, they were concerned with agricultural technology; but because what they had read of the subject pertained mainly to England, they had little success in applying their information. Nevertheless, they successfully introduced, by trial and error, a variety of new plants into Virginia. By 1773 the colony's foremost citizens were strongly enough interested in scientific and other intellectual pursuits to induce the governor to establish, in Williamsburg, a philosophical society for the advancement of useful knowledge in the colony. The society enlisted a hundred members.

In the course of and following the American Revolution, a number of Virginia's leaders took advantage of opportunities to give guidance to the political thinking of the state and nation. These leaders articulated various political theories, discussed state and national constitutional issues, and formulated state and national legislative programs. One can better appreciate the quality of their leadership in political thought by recalling that the framer of the Declaration of Independence, one of the three authors of *The Federalist Papers,* and the nation's first chief justice were all Virginians. But Virginia's learned citizens did not become wholly absorbed in politics. They maintained their interest in the classics and English writers, continued their small scientific endeavors, and expanded their reading in French philosophy.

The dominant principle of educational finance in colonial Virginia was voluntarism. Education was to be available to those who, under the aegis of their parents, wanted it and could afford it. In other words, private education was the rule; and needless to say, the principle was popular among the planters, who, as the colony's major tax payers, would have had to pay the bulk of the expenses for a general system of public education. The outcome of Virginia's educational financial policy was that the upper classes received a substantial education and, thereby, were prepared to enter the professions and businesses and assume positions of leadership, whereas the lower classes received, at best, just enough education to assume the tasks of skilled labor.[13]

The education undertaken by students from the landed aristocracy served to prepare them for participation in the leisure pursuits of their class, to enable them to enter the legal profession and take part in political affairs, to give them skills especially useful in managing lands, and to provide them with religious training. The first two of these functions were served through a strong curriculum in literary studies, namely, English, Latin, Greek, and French. Skill in land management was developed through a study of some relatively advanced mathematics and surveying. And the religious training was provided through catechetical instruction and religious exercises. Normally, a student from the landed aristocracy obtained his primary schooling on his father's plantation from a tutor. For his secondary schooling, he either had the services of a tutor or left the plantation to room and board at an academy, which might have been at the house of his teacher. Often the primary and secondary teachers were Anglican clergymen seeking to supplement their incomes. If the student desired further liberal education, he usually attended Oxford or Cambridge or William and Mary. (The latter, under the aegis of the Anglican Church and situated in Williamsburg, gave a higher liberal education, trained ministers, furnished Christian instruction to a few Indians, and offered secondary schooling.) To prepare himself for the legal profession, the student might have studied at the Inns of Court in London or under a Virginia practitioner.

Although generally unable to afford tutors, the merchants and more prosperous shopkeeper families did send their children to academies, which usually were not those attended by students from the aristocracy. At the academies the burgher family students received, in addition to religious training, instruction in English, Latin, Italian, French, geography, and practical mathematics. These studies had a distinct possible vocational value. While the literary studies obviously prepared the students to participate in gentlemanly leisure pursuits, they also prepared them to carry on the great amount of correspondence involved in business, including communications with non-English-speaking Europeans. Mathematics helped teach the students to keep books and post bills, and geography acquainted them with economic aspects of the earth. After finishing their schooling, most of these students immediately entered the business world; but some attended William and Mary to read law.

The less prosperous shopkeepers and the craftsmen, who were hardly ever prosperous, were able to afford only a few years of schooling for their children, during which the latter learned the elements of religion, English, and arithmetic. Not all of these shopkeepers and craftsmen, however, were able to afford this much. Some simply set their children to learning a trade, usually through apprenticeship. Sometimes a master assumed responsibility not only for teaching an apprentice a trade but also for obtaining for him some schooling in reading, writing, and ciphering. Those parents who did send their children to school saw to it that, afterwards, they began to learn a trade. Often the children of small farmers went without schooling and apprenticing. Out of respect for education, a few wealthy colonials had endowed schools for indigent children; but these schools were very rare, and probably no more than six were ever in operation at one time. To ensure that pauper children, who had no responsible parents, would not remain social burdens, the House of Burgesses had passed laws requiring local communities to set out such children to apprenticeship and to secure them instruction in religion, reading, writing, and ciphering.

During and after the American Revolution, efforts were made to provide a general system of publicly financed education in Virginia; but these were defeated. Most of the state's wealthy citizens were still opposed to paying the taxes needed to support the schooling of the poor. However, higher education in the state was strengthened with a reorganization of the curriculum of William and Mary, and, much later, with the founding of the University of Virginia.

· NOTES ·

1. Thomas J. Wertenbaker, *The Planters of Colonial Virginia* (Princeton, N.J.: Princeton University Press, 1922), pp. 52–54.
2. Richard L. Morton, *Colonial Virginia* (Chapel Hill: The University of North Carolina Press, 1960), II, Chaps. 13, 14.
3. *Ibid.*, p. 824.
4. Wertenbaker, *op. cit.*, pp. 55–56, 130–131.
5. Cf. Freeman H. Hart, *The Valley of Virginia in the American Revolution, 1763–1789* (Chapel Hill: The University of North Carolina Press, 1942), pp. 98 ff., 111 ff.
6. Cf. *ibid.*, Chap. 7.
7. Cf. Philip A. Bruce, *Institutional History of Virginia in the Seventeenth Century* (New York: Putnam, 1910), II, Chaps. 9, 11. Morton, *op. cit.*, Chaps. 1, 2.
8. Cf. Bruce, *op. cit.*, Chaps. 13, 15. Morton, *op. cit.*, pp. 411–415.
9. Cf. Bruce, *op. cit.*, Chaps. 22, 27, 28, 29. Morton, *op. cit.*, pp. 430–431, 455–560, 502–506, 627–630.
10. Hart, *op. cit.*, pp. 120–123.
11. Cf. Thomas J. Wertenbaker, *The Old South* (New York: Scribner, 1942), pp. 10–11.
12. See *ibid.*, Chap. 2.
13. Cf. Newton Edwards and H. G. Richey, *The School in the American Social Order*, 2nd ed. (Boston: Houghton Mifflin, 1963), pp. 131 ff.

· III ·
The Influence of the Historical Milieu

The economic, political, social, and cultural forces of Jefferson's historical milieu helped to determine his philosophical ideas and educational proposals by providing the sources of the ideas and proposals and by furnishing the conditions in response to which his thoughts were conceived. By learning the sources of influence on Jefferson's thought, one will be able to gain insights into the meanings of a few of Jefferson's ideas and proposals that he did not explain very well and to discern the relationship between his practical educational proposals and his philosophical ideas and theoretical educational proposals.

I

Jefferson's birthplace was Shadwell, the comfortable but simple plantation residence of his father, Peter. It was located in the piedmont region a few miles across the Rivanna River from where Monticello stands. Although Peter Jefferson was not from a distinguished family and had not been formally educated beyond the secondary level, he was definitely a member of Virginia's landed gentry.[1] By the time of his death, he owned between 7,000 and 10,000 acres of land, more than sixty slaves, and several hundred head of livestock. He had held the positions of justice of the peace, sheriff, and county surveyor of Virginia for the Crown; and, also by Crown appointment, he had been a co-draftsman of a map of the uninhabited parts of the colony. Finally, he had established intimate connections with the illustrious Randolph family. For instance, he had served as executor of the estate of William Randolph, who had been his close friend, and, in October 1739, he had married Isham Randolph's daughter Jane.

Having been born into colonial Virginia's aristocracy, Thomas Jefferson, during his early years, participated widely in the richer elements of the colony's culture. And, in so doing, he underwent experiences which contributed to his philosophical and educational thought. Some of these experiences will now be discussed.

At the age of five he began his primary schooling. The record, which is not very clear, does indicate that he received instruction in the fundamentals of the English language and arithmetic. It is likely that he was also given instruction in the Anglican religion during this period. At the age of nine he entered the secondary school conducted by Reverend William Douglas, where he studied mainly Latin, Greek, and French. But he seems not to have been taught at least some of these languages very well, for in later years he noted that Douglas knew Latin only superficially and Greek even less.

When only fourteen, Jefferson suffered the death of his father and became a principal heir to his father's estate. In addition to land, slaves, and livestock (which he was not to control until he attained his majority), he inherited some of his father's smaller possessions, including mathematical instruments and a few books. Whether or not he ever made much use of the instruments is not known; but that he later became quite interested in mathematics and drafting—both architectural and mechanical—suggests the influence of his father. The books, on a variety of topics, proved to be the beginning of the first of three libraries assembled by Jefferson.

Despite his father's death Jefferson had a fortunate change in his fourteenth year, for he entered the secondary school directed by the Reverend James Maury. Although this man, staunchly Anglican and intolerant of dissenting sects, seems not to have left his stamp on Jefferson's religious beliefs, he appears to have laid the basis of Jefferson's strong and abiding interest in the classics. By the end of the two years that he spent at Maury's school, Jefferson was reading, in the original, major Greek and Latin authors, a practice that was to become a lifelong habit with him. Even in his late years he referred to Maury as "a correct scholar." It is possible that Maury, who had a large library, a fine English style, and decided opinions on literary study in general, was also the one who engendered Jefferson's interest in modern literature.

Toward the end of his stay at Maury's school, Jefferson decided to continue his education at William and Mary, where, he assumed, he could pursue his studies in Greek and Latin, "learn something of the Mathematics," and "get a more universal Acquaintance." [2] He enrolled in what was called the philosophy curriculum, which included natural philosophy (mathematics, physics, and metaphysics) and moral philosophy (logic, ethics, rhetoric, and belles-lettres).

Although the faculty of William and Mary included six clergymen, it generally failed to provide a model of moral and intellectual virtue. President Dawson, who died during the course of Jefferson's first year at the college, was well known as an excessive drinker, and his sober successor was a dull teacher. On several occasions, lesser clerical faculty members led students in scrapes with Williamsburg's youth. None of the clerical faculty seems to have shown the marks of sound scholarship. So, even though Jefferson did attend church while going to college, he was not morally and intellectually led by the clergy. Such guidance came, rather, from William Small, the single lay member of the faculty, who, according to Jefferson, probably fixed the destinies of the younger man's life. Having arrived at William and Mary from England in 1760 (the same year that Jefferson came there), Small taught, at first, the courses in natural philosophy and, later, those in moral philosophy. He was, Jefferson wrote, "a man profound in most of the useful branches of science, with a happy talent of communication correct and gentlemanly manners, and an enlarged and liberal mind." [3] Jefferson took most of his courses under Small, and he also learned much from him through the friendship that developed between them. Perhaps finding in Jefferson a kindred spirit, Small soon became attached to him and made him his daily companion. Jefferson notes that from his conversations with Small he obtained his first views of "the expansion of science and of the system of things in which we are placed." [4]

Small had friends other than Jefferson in Williamsburg, the most notable of whom were George Wythe and Francis Fauquier. Wythe, who was proficient in Greek and Latin and largely self-taught in his profession, was one of Virginia's leading lawyers and a member of the House of Burgesses. Fauquier, who was keenly interested in the arts and natural philosophy, was the colony's lieutenant governor. Small introduced both of these men to Jefferson, who, by the end of his college days, was accepted by them as a friend. Jefferson sometimes joined Small and Wythe at Fauquier's for dinner and conversation and attended other social gatherings at the governor's mansion. There is little doubt that the youthful Jefferson gained intellectual stimulation as well as enjoyment from such splendid company. His visits to the lieutenant governor's home also gave Jefferson an opportunity to observe fine manners and elegant surroundings that he had not known in the piedmont area.

After two years of college, Jefferson, at the age of nineteen, began his five years of reading in law.[5] Taking lodgings in Williamsburg, he pursued his legal studies under Wythe's supervision. His basic texts were those making up the *Institutes of the Lawes of England,* which, far from being a philosophical treatment of law, were primarily an exposition of English law, including Coke's rigorous and pedantic explication of the terms found in early English law. Jefferson also read several volumes of English court cases and the collected statutes of Virginia. In his study of English legal institutions, he became cognizant of the Anglo-Saxon origin of the administrative unit called the "hundred" (a county sub-division), which he later used as a guide in planning the administration of his proposed system of public education for Virginia.

Jefferson worked diligently at his legal studies, but he certainly did not lose himself in them. Indeed, finding himself on the threshold of manhood, he heartily entered the life of the young squire. He went to the horse races on the outskirts of Williamsburg, to plays at the town's theater, and to dances held in the Apollo room of the town's Raleigh tavern. Having become fairly accomplished on the violin, he played in amateur chamber music groups at the governor's mansion. And he experienced his first romance, which ended in disappointment for him. Although Jefferson was responsible to Wythe for his legal preparation, he spent a large part of his time, after his first year, at Shadwell, which was fitting for one intending to be a planter as well as a lawyer.

Despite the demands of his professional preparation and the activeness of his social life, Jefferson persisted in his liberal education. He no longer had the scholarly guidance of Small, who had returned to England shortly after Jefferson had begun reading law. But he had access to the advice of Wythe on classical literature and, perhaps, that of Fauquier on modern philosophy and literature. An examination of the literary notebook which he kept reveals that between 1764 and 1772 he carefully read, at least in part, works by Homer, Herodotus, Euripides, Cicero, Vergil, Terence, Shakespeare, Milton, Pope, Bolingbroke, and others.[6] He read the classical authors in the original but included Pope's translation of Homer. In spite of its copiousness, the literary notebook must not be regarded as containing a full roster of the philosophers and poets whom Jefferson read during this period. By his own testimony[7] he read, at this time, Lord Kames, who is not mentioned in the notebook.

A large portion of the elements in Jefferson's youthful experience of Virginia's culture were later to be reflected in his specific recommendations for secondary and collegiate curricula. One of the more noticeable elements can be found in the nonreligious orientation that he assigned to moral instruction. When a student, he found a moral model not in any clergyman but in Small. And, according to the passages in his literary notebook, he found poetry and philosophy but not the Bible to be sources of moral precepts. When he eventually formulated his educational thought, he proposed that moral education could be effectively provided without a religious framework.

The factors in Jefferson's early experience that contributed to his philosophical ideas certainly included some of the writings which he read during his stay at college and his legal studies. Among the passages that Jefferson copied into his literary notebook, there may be found terms and statements suggestive of some that appear in the philosophical position which he assumed in his mature years. For example, Bolingbroke's principles of matter and reason are indicative of the similar principles that Jefferson came to hold firmly. And the statements of stoical wisdom by Seneca, for example, anticipate the prudential rules that Jefferson was to advocate in his later ethical writings. Moreover, it is important to remember that Jefferson claims to have read at this time Lord Kames, who apparently had a distinct bearing on Jefferson's political and moral views (as will be subsequently specified).

One should not conclude, however, that the elements of Jefferson's early experience of Virginia's culture influenced his educational or philosophical views in a neat way. Each element influenced his ideas only insofar as it intermixed with factors entering his life after his student years.

II

In early 1767, when he became a practicing lawyer, Jefferson was a minor figure in the colony's aristocracy, but in less than a decade he was a leader of the American Revolution. During this period of early adulthood, he continued to indulge in serious study; but he also encountered conditions in response to which he articulated his political thought and many of his recommendations on education.

Jefferson pursued the legal profession for only seven years. He had to stop practicing when, because of revolutionary stirrings, Virginia's courts closed. He never returned to the profession, probably because of his involvement in politics. Two events in his legal career, however, deserve special notice. It was as a lawyer that Jefferson is first known to have expressed an opinion regarding education for someone other than himself.[8] Asked by an uncle to accept the latter's son as an apprentice in the study of law, Jefferson declined on the ground that he did not have the time to do the favor; but he also gave a strong criticism of the apprentice system of education in law, namely, that lawyers were prone to shift much of their work onto their apprentices and, in so doing, encroach upon the time that the latter should devote to their studies. Moreover, it was as a lawyer that Jefferson is first known to have argued the principles of natural law and right and to have expressed an opinion on the plight of the Negro in Virginia.[9] Early in his career he took, without fee, the case of Samuel Howell, a mulatto who had been placed in bondage because he had been born to a mulatto bond servant. Jefferson contended, without success, that his client had been wrongly put into servitude; and he argued on the ground that his client had not been born into such a state because, among other reasons, all men by nature are born free.

At the same time that he was engaged in his law practice, Jefferson was also devoting much attention to his domestic life.[10] Upon attaining his majority, he had taken as his major inheritance his father's holdings along the Rivanna River; and soon afterward he showed signs of being an earnest planter. In 1769 he began the work on Monticello, which proved to be a fortunate project for him. Shadwell, where Jefferson had continued living with his mother, several of his sisters, and his brother, was extensively damaged by fire early in 1770. But in the fall of that year one of the outbuildings on the Monticello site was sufficiently completed so that Jefferson was able to move into it. After his marriage, in 1772, to Martha Wayles Skelton, a widow whom he had likely met in Williamsburg, he probably brought his bride to this dwelling.

Despite the demands of his professional and domestic life, Jefferson broadened his reading, especially in philosophy and history. By the beginning of his legal practice, he had acquainted himself with some of the writings of Francis Bacon, whom he later ranked with Isaac Newton and John Locke as a member of his intellectual trinity. And in 1769, the year of his admission to the House of

Burgesses and the year before the Howell case, he placed an order for Locke's essays on government, Montesquieu's works, Burlamaque's *Le droit naturel,* some histories of civil wars, and other works of political significance.[11] Having lost nearly all of his books in the Shadwell fire, he began his second library shortly afterward by more than doubling the number of volumes of the first.

By the time he was established at Monticello, Jefferson had taken obvious directions in his theoretical thinking. His apparent interest in Bolingbroke suggested a leaning toward materialism, the belief that anything which exists is material in some sense; and his perusal of Bacon in addition to Bolingbroke intimated a taste for empiricism, the belief that any knowledge of any existing thing depends upon sensory experience. Because, during his student years, Jefferson had rejected established Christianity as a source of morality, he sought a suitable alternative. At first he favored a kind of stoicism, which he appears to have relied upon mainly as a defense against the troubles of his youthful romance.[12] Subsequently, he became impressed with Kames' ethical theory and seemed inclined toward a moral sense doctrine, that is, a position holding that men naturally possess a moral sense which tells them the difference between right and wrong.[13] During the period of his legal training, Jefferson seems not to have studied much political philosophy; but what he studied appears to have helped to direct his later pursuits in that field. At least some of what he read was Kames' *Historical Law Tracts,* which provided him with an examination of English law within the framework of natural law.[14] On the occasion of his entering the House of Burgesses, he sought to further his understanding of natural law theory, but the fact that Jefferson held, at this stage, some recognizable theoretical views does not mean that he had clearly defined them to himself. In fact, he was to work at the clarification of these ideas during much of the remainder of his life. In response to demanding circumstances, he was to develop his political ideas before his educational ones.

Jefferson's venture into politics had several roots: his interest in law, his acquaintance with Wythe and Fauquier, his father's example, and his membership in Virginia's landed gentry. The venture began in December 1768, when he was elected to the House of Burgesses (where he was to hold his seat, except when he attended the Continental Congress, until he became governor during the revolution). When he left for Williamsburg in the spring of 1769, he was alert to the comparatively new features in the colony's political situation. Fauquier had died and a resident governor had been appointed. The leadership of the House of Burgesses was still held by Peyton Randolph, Edmund Pendleton, Robert Carter Nicholas, and other older members; but the "old guard" was being challenged by some younger members, chiefly, Patrick Henry. The issue that initially prompted the challenge was whether or not England had the right to impose an internal tax on Virginians. In 1764, when the Stamp Tax bill was being debated in Parliament, virtually all members of the House of Burgesses stoutly opposed the bill's passage. After the tax became law, however, the dominant members, not desiring rebellion in the colony, deemed it wise to comply. But when Henry, before the General Assembly in 1765, vociferously attacked the Stamp Tax law as unjust and unworthy of compliance, he upset whatever complacency the leaders may have had about Virginia's relations with England. Although his position was generally thought too radical then, it did instigate a rethinking of the colony's position of subservience. Jefferson had been impressed by Henry's speech, and after entering the assembly, he sided mainly with the "young Turks."

The first year of Jefferson's legislative career proved exciting. The immediate issue was the Townshend duties, which appeared to the colonials to be a violation of their right to control their internal affairs. In contrast with its reaction to the Stamp Tax, the General Assembly did not acquiesce when faced with the Townshend duties. First, although avowing its loyalty to the Crown, it passed a resolution declaring that the Burgesses and not Parliament had the right to tax the colony. Then, after the General Assembly was dissolved by the governor because of the resolution, a large number of the members, including Peyton Randolph and others of the "old guard," drew up and signed a nonimportation-nonconsumption agreement. This was the first notable public paper that Jefferson signed. In 1770, after all of the duties except that on tea had been rescinded, a large group of Burgesses (including Jefferson) and local merchants drew up and signed another nonimportation-nonconsumption agreement. By the end of the year, however, this group had lost its enthusiasm; and rebellious activities subsided until 1773.

By that year the *Gaspee* incident in Rhode Island had raised afresh the issue of whether or not a colonial could rightfully be taken to England for trial. As a result, Jefferson, Patrick Henry, and other activists decided that a unity of colonial action was needed and framed and submitted to Virginia's legislature a resolution calling for committees of correspondence. The resolution was passed and the assembly was prorogued. When the Burgesses gathered in the spring of the next year, they knew about the Boston Tea Party and the Port Act imposed upon that city; and they regarded the situation in Massachusetts as an occasion for arousing public feeling against England. Jefferson was chosen to draft a resolution for a day of fasting and prayer to mark the closing of Boston Harbor.[15] After the resolution was passed, the governor dissolved the General Assembly in hope of getting a more agreeable House of Burgesses elected; but the day of fasting and prayer was widely observed in the colony. Immediately following the dissolution, the Burgesses' committee of correspondence met and decided that measures must be taken to convene a congress of the colonies; and shortly afterward a convention of Burgesses assembled in Williamsburg. Jefferson was ill and could not attend, but he sent to the convention a resolution he had drafted that proposed instructions to Virginia's delegates to the forthcoming Continental Congress.[16] The resolution was never officially acted upon but was soon published in Williamsburg under the title, *A Summary View of the Rights of British America*, which was the first of Jefferson's popularly acclaimed writings. It had been closely preceded by several other pieces of his political writings, but the resolution may be regarded as epitomizing his political thought at this time.

In his resolution Jefferson contended that, although the colonials owed obedience to the monarchy, they were in no way subject to Parliament. To support his claim, he appealed to the doctrine of natural rights: following their God-given rights, the colonials had chosen to leave England, where they had been citizens merely by chance, and had chosen to form new societies in America to attain their happiness; and, according to natural law and right, they and they alone possessed the right to make laws concerning their affairs (including their foreign commerce). In the argument happiness is plainly made the end of political society. Two natural rights are made explicit: the right of a person to belong to the society of his choice and the right of self-government. The right of revolution, the public base of authority, and a contract theory of government are alluded to; but there is no explicit preference for democracy. At this stage of his life, Jefferson disavowed all forms of tyranny but had no fundamental objections to monarchy or aristocracy.

In late spring of 1775, following the engagements at Lexington and Concord, Jefferson went as a delegate to the Continental Congress in Philadelphia. Because he was already distinguished as a penman, he was called upon to write several papers. One that he drafted (but that was not adopted) was a declaration on the causes and necessity of taking up arms.[17] The point of the declaration was that the English government had given the colonials just cause for armed rebellion. To support his contention, Jefferson relied upon principles of natural right that he had previously employed; but he also explicitly appealed to a contract theory of government: the king had seriously violated his "charters of compact" with the colonies and, thereby, had relieved them of their obligations to the monarch. But this declaration did not contain the whole framework of what was to be Jefferson's political philosophy. The whole was not to be assembled until the following year, when he wrote the Declaration of Independence.

During 1775 the fighting between the colonials and the British was confined to the North, but in the early part of 1776 it broke out in Virginia. As a result, most of the leaders of the colony who had continued to hope for a reconciliation with England shortly abandoned that project and joined with those who thought that independence from England was desirable. In May the Burgesses instructed Virginia's delegation at the Continental Congress to press for a declaration of independence, and by early June the Congress appointed a committee to draw up such a declaration. Benjamin Franklin, John Adams, Roger Sherman, Robert R. Livingston, and Jefferson constituted the committee; and Jefferson was designated to do the original draft, which he worked on June 11–28. His purpose was to justify the colonies' decision to become independent, but he was not satisfied with simply stating the particular grievances that the colonies held against the Crown. He also wanted to provide these grievances with a theoretical ground. To this end he set forth a succinct but systematic and comprehesive statement of the principles of natural law theory:

> When in the course of human events it becomes necessary for a people to advance from that subordination in which they have hitherto remained, & to assume among the powers of the earth the equal & independant station to which the laws of nature & of nature's god entitle them, a decent respect to the opinions of mankind requires that they should declare the causes which impel them to the change.

> *We hold these truths to be sacred & undeniable; that all men are created equal & independent, that from that equal creation they derive rights inherent & inalienable, among which are the preservation of life, & liberty, & the pursuit of happiness; that to secure these ends, governments are instituted among men, deriving their just powers from the consent of the governed; that whenever any form of government shall become destructive of these ends, it is the right of the people to alter or to abolish it, & to institute new government, laying it's foundation on such principles & organising it's powers in such form, as to them shall seem most likely to effect their safety & happiness.*[18]

Although Jefferson's fundamental political principles contained in the Declaration of Independence are expressed rather vaguely, some of them may be clarified. In saying that all men are created equal and independent, Jefferson apparently intended the word "men" to include Negroes as well as Caucasians. It will be recalled that in the Howell case he argued that *all* men by nature are born free. Moreover, in his proposed constitution for Virginia,[19] which he drew up just prior to beginning work on the Declaration of Independence, he called for an end to the colony's slave trade (which was the only feature of Virginia's slavery institution that he thought could feasibly be abolished at this time). In saying that all men have inherent and inalienable rights, he had in mind more than life, liberty, and the pursuit of happiness, because his proposed constitution for Virginia (adopted only in part) included a lengthy bill of rights, which specified, among others, the freedom of religion and press. And, in saying that governments derive their just powers from the governed, he included the principle of majority rule. His proposed constitution for Virginia called for a direct popular election of a house of representatives, which would elect a senate and an executive. Furthermore, in a letter commenting upon his proposed constitution,[20] Jefferson stated that the right to vote must be extended to any freeman who gave evidence (ownership of a minimal amount of land) that he intended to reside in Virginia. By the middle of 1776, then, Jefferson had developed a democratic political theory, or what he preferred to call a "republican" political theory. What ultimately led him to such a theory is not apparent. No doubt, the increasingly hostile action by the British Crown turned him against monarchy; but what moved him against aristocracy and toward democracy is not certain. Perhaps it was resentment toward the power of the tidewater aristocracy or Jefferson's reading of the logic of natural rights. Whatever else it may have been it was not class interest: as an aristocrat, Jefferson stood to gain nothing by supporting democracy.

While Jefferson's theoretical political position was plainly shaped, to an important extent, by the natural law theories he had studied, his theories must not be viewed as a reproduction of any particular one of them. For example, Jefferson did borrow, indirectly (through Kames and others) or directly, Locke's ideas of natural law and right and the political compact; but he certainly did not accept Locke's theory *in toto*. Jefferson gave a prominent place to the pursuit of happiness as a natural right, whereas Locke never regarded it as a natural right. Jefferson defined liberty as unobstructed willful action, whether that action conforms with natural law or not; whereas Locke viewed it as willful action that accords with natural law. And Jefferson stoutly propounded the political necessity for a complete separation between church and government, whereas Locke looked upon a government-supported church, bound by a policy of toleration toward dissenting sects, as politically acceptable.[21]

A few months after he had completed the Declaration of Independence, Jefferson resigned from the Continental Congress and took a seat in the Virginia legislature. He wanted to be near his family, and he desired to help assure that the new state would be organized according to republican principles. In view of the latter aim, he saw the legislature's job as twofold: to eradicate every fiber of "antient or future aristocracy" and to lay a foundation for a government "truly republican." He had an excellent opportunity to promote his ideas; for, along with George Wythe and Edmund Pendleton, he was assigned the task of revising the whole corpus of Virginia's laws. Of the many bills that he wrote during his relatively brief career as a state legislator, he regarded four as cardinal.[22] The bill repealing the laws of entail and that abolishing primogeniture eliminated two notable property institutions of aristocratic Virginia. The bill establishing religious freedom did away with the privileged position of the Anglican Church. And the bill for general education, submitted in 1779, was intended to enable the poor to understand their rights and to participate intelligently in self-government. The first three bills, while opposed in some quarters, were passed; but the last was rejected. As Jefferson surmised, Virginia's rich were generally not willing to pay for the education of the state's poor.

Although Jefferson thought the general education bill was quite important, he submitted to the Virginia legislature two other bills concerning education, which were also

rejected. The general education bill provided for a syst
of primary schools and for one of secondary schools.[23] The
primary schools, which were to teach reading, writing,
common arithmetic, and history, were to be free to all.
And the secondary schools, which were to teach Latin,
Greek, English, geography, and a relatively advanced
arithmetic, were to be free to only the best of the indigent
students. The most talented of the impoverished secondary school students were to be given a free college education. Another bill proposed that the College of William
and Mary be taken over by the state and reorganized in
both administration and curriculum.[24] The curriculum
was to be altered to exclude theology and to include
ethics, fine arts, law, history, mathematics, anatomy and
medicine, natural philosophy and history, and ancient and
modern languages. The third bill provided for a publicly
financed library of books and maps to be used by the
"learned and curious." [25]

One factor that induced Jefferson to perceive and
focus on the importance of education for a democratic society was the study he had devoted to political philosophy.
During his reading of political theorists, he, without question, had become aware of the point that a state of a given
kind needs citizens of a certain type and can best obtain
them through appropriate education. In what work Jefferson had first encountered this idea and in what books he
subsequently studied it is not determinable. It is undeniable, however, that he had taken notice of it during his
study of Montesquieu of whom he wrote:

> *He considers political virtue or the Amor Patriae as the*
> *energetic principle of a democratic republic; moderation,*

*that of an aristocratic republic; honor, that of a limited
monarchy; and fear, that of a despotism; and shews
that every government should provide that it's energetic
principle should be the object of the education of it's
youth.*[26]

According to Jefferson's political theory, the purpose of a
democracy is to enable its citizens to exercise their natural
rights and, thereby, obtain happiness; and this purpose
suggests that the aim of education in any democratic society is to provide the society's members with the knowledge and skills that will enable them to know and exercise
their natural rights in both the public and private sections
of this society. Moreover, the citizens of a democracy need
leaders who have superior intelligence and moral virtue.
Consequently, the function of education in a democratic
state is threefold: to furnish all citizens with the knowledge and training that will enable them to pursue happiness as private persons; to prepare all citizens to exercise
their rights of self-government; and to provide the knowledge and training that will enable the superiorly gifted
citizens to make full use of their intellectual and moral
powers, especially with respect to the exigencies of leadership. Jefferson apparently had these objectives in mind
when he wrote his general education bill. The schooling
which was to be free for all citizens of Virginia was essential to the exercise of their natural rights. And the complete formal education, which was to be offered free to the
superior impecunious students, was obviously meant to
help assure that Virginia would have citizens qualified to
be leaders. Furthermore, Jefferson apparently had in view
the objective of preparing citizens to be leaders when he
drew up the bill, concerning William and Mary, which

proposed a curriculum appropriate for training people to be leaders in the private sector (mainly, the economy and professions), as well as the public sector (chiefly, the government) of Virginia. Finally, Jefferson was probably thinking about the desirability of continuing the education of those qualified to be leaders in a democracy when he framed the bill for establishing a public library. Envisioned as an institution to serve the "learned and curious" (not the general public), the library was seemingly intended to be a facility whereby the well educated might continue to increase their knowledge and, thereby, gain insight for maintaining the natural rights of Virginia's citizenry.

Although it was the case, presumably, that Jefferson's political theory was reflected in his suggestions for an educational program, it must not be thought that the program's substantive features were suggested to him by the theory. They were intimated by the given conditions of colonial Virginia. The economic system, which fostered a huge body of poor people, necessitated a program including a publicly financed general system of education. The curricular offerings of colonial Virginia, which provided no civic instruction to the mass of its students, which included religious indoctrination and exercises, and which provided few utilitarian studies at the collegiate level, indicated an obvious need for a program advancing a curriculum more relevant to Virginia as a democratic society. And the fact that Virginia's libraries were all in private hands showed the desirability of a program containing a public institution of research materials.

III

In 1779 and again in the following year, Thomas Jefferson was elected governor of Virginia. Holding the office when the fighting of the American Revolution was largely located in the southern colonies, he decided to forego attempts at democratic reform and to concentrate on the state's military needs. During the course of his second term, he faced strong political criticism: chiefly, he was accused of not providing an adequate defense for Virginia against the British forces. Although the charges were largely unfounded, he resigned from office and retired briefly to Monticello from public affairs. In the years that followed, elements of his historical situation continued to affect the development of his philosophical ideas and educational proposals. A few elements had long been familiar to him, and others were new. Some of the new ones were eighteenth-century French natural philosophy, the moral teachings of Jesus, and the theology of Joseph Priestley.

When Jefferson retired in 1781, he turned his mind and energy to a scholarly project, the writing of his book *Notes on the State of Virginia*. The work consists of Jefferson's answers to twenty-three queries on diverse features of Virginia. The questions had been sent to him by a member of the French legation at Philadelphia who was seeking information for his government on the American states. In the work Jefferson examined the institution of slavery; and, in so doing, he somewhat clarified his view of human nature and suggested some principles of learning.

During his analysis of the institution, he took up the issue of the place of the Negro in Virginia.[27] First of all, he argued fervently that slavery was wrong. It violated the natural rights belonging to the Negroes as human beings. Furthermore, slavery encouraged a tyrannical disposition in the members of the slave-owning class. Next, he pointed out that, although the majority of Virginia's citizens were not ready to accept a policy of emancipation, the sentiment for such a policy was definitely growing. Last, he made a proposal on the status of the Negro in Virginia after emancipation: rather than continuing to live in Virginia, the freed slaves, after being prepared for self-government, should be deported to a land (perhaps the frontier) where they could establish a society of their own. Jefferson founded this proposal on two premises. (1) If the freed slaves remained in Virginia, they might rise up in a fierce rebellion to redress the wrongs that had been done to them. (2) If they stayed in Virginia, they might intermarry with the Caucasian citizens and, thereby, cause the degeneration of the state's citizenry. This premise, implying a natural inferiority of the Negro to the Caucasian race, was advanced by Jefferson with grave reservations. He stressed that his evidence for the supposed inferiority of the Negro race came from nothing more than his own observations. And he emphasized that it was extremely difficult to evaluate the innate qualities of any human being because they are not open to direct inspection. Thus, he regarded the premise as simply a suspicion, a notion to be accepted or rejected on the ground of further and more adequate empirical investigation.

To a large extent Jefferson discussed this issue in terms of human nature. It is not known definitely where he had located these principles, but it may be presumed that he had become acquainted with them in his study of

English philosophy. According to Jefferson, human nature consists of psychological faculties, namely, reason, moral sense, taste, imagination, memory, appetites, passions, and the five senses. Although these faculties are innate in human beings, they exist in stronger or weaker degrees among individual men. For example, all men naturally possess reason; but some have greater rational powers than others. Consequently, some students may not learn as much or as well as other students. Although the powers of reason, moral sense, imagination, and memory are present at birth, they are unformed then and must be developed through exercise. And because the environment significantly determines the exercise of these faculties, it has a notable bearing on the formation of the self. Hence, learning is related to the student's environment. Finally, different faculties are appropriate to different subject matters. For example, science is primarily the province of reason; morals belong chiefly to the moral sense; and art pertains mainly to taste. Curricula may be departmentalized accordingly.

In the fall of 1783, about a year after the death of his wife, Jefferson went to the Continental Congress as a delegate from Virginia; and the following summer he left for France, where he was to reside for five years as an ambassador to that nation. During the period of his new public life, he found what proved to be a fresh source of ideas: eighteenth-century French natural philosophy.[28] To be sure, he had read Buffon, Raynal, and other writers in the field before he had written his *Notes*; but he became more interested in such philosophy (which was not well-known in Virginia) when he was ambassador to France. While in that nation, where he was well received, he made the acquaintance of Condorcet, La Rochefoucauld, Cabanis, Destutt de Tracy, and others. He purchased, for his friends in America as well as for himself, a vast quantity of books concerning current French philosophical thought. And he acquainted himself with practices that this thought had fostered, notably, scientific agriculture and agricultural education. However, it must be noted that, while he was in France, he met and was impressed by Dugald Stewart, a Scottish moral sense philosopher—a point which suggests that, although he was influenced by French natural philosophy, he did not abandon his previously held theory of nature but came to adopt those principles of French natural philosophy that he found helpful in developing this theory. Like Jefferson, eighteenth-century French philosophers were materialists and empiricists, but unlike Jefferson, a number of them were atheists and thought that morality was not based in nature but was a human convention.

Although Jefferson was abroad when the American Constitutional Convention was in session, he endeavored to keep himself informed of its actions; and, in correspondence on several constitutional issues, he took the opportunity to explicate various of his political principles, especially his contract view of government. Soon after returning to America, he entered into the service of the newly founded federal government as George Washington's Secretary of State; and he was not to leave national office, except during a pair of brief interims, until the end of his second term as President in 1809. Throughout the long course of his national public service, he had much opportunity to follow his intellectual interests. He addressed himself to a great many national problems; and, in examining and guiding his investigations of them, he made use of and further clarified his theoretical principles.[29] Witnessing the numerous political attacks on and by the press, he passionately expounded the right of the freedom of the press.[30] Moreover, Jefferson found some leisure in which to entertain questions removed from the political sphere. In correspondence with the Pennsylvania physician Benjamin Rush, he compared and contrasted classic, Judaic, and Christian moralities with one another.[31] And, in a letter to the English theologian and scientist Joseph Priestley, he discussed the value of the study of Latin and Greek.[32] Although Jefferson was able to follow many of his intellectual interests—theoretical and practical—during this period of national service, he did not scrutinize his fundamental philosophical ideas; and he did very little toward formulating educational measures.

After leaving national office, Jefferson gave up his regular participation in public affairs and stayed mainly at Monticello, though he certainly did not become a recluse. He received numerous visitors, including some notables from abroad, and proffered advice to Presidents Madison and Monroe whenever they sought it. After the British burned Washington during the War of 1812, he sold nearly all of his library collection (about 10,000 books) to the federal government to replace the Congressional Library, which had been destroyed, and soon began building up his third collection. More importantly, he resumed consideration of his basic philosophical ideas and endeavored to promote public education in Virginia.

Ever since his student days, when he had taken to Newtonian physics and read Bolingbroke, Jefferson had intimated a predilection for the postulate that all existing things are material and explicable in terms of experience. However, he had not, as far as anyone knows, comprehensively examined the postulate before the waning years of his life. When he turned, in his late years, to a perusal of several eighteenth-century French philosophers, he encountered serious discussions of the materialist-empiricist position; and he was guided by them, seemingly, in specifying and ordering his own, less clearly defined, notions of materialism and empiricism. Thus, he concluded that all existing things are material, that whatever is not material does not exist, and that the seats of the psychological faculties are corporeal organs. In addition, he connected his materialism with his empiricism: any knowledge of any existing thing depends upon sensory experience. Beyond this connection his empiricism held that the senses can perceive particular things but never anything in general. For instance, one can have a sensory experience of this or that man but not human nature. General ideas, or forms, are products of reason grounded on sense experience. Jefferson seems not to have noticed the difficulties (which will be mentioned subsequently) involved in his empiricist position when it is related to his natural law theory, but he did directly relate materialism to his principle of God. Rejecting the atheism of Diderot, d'Holbach, and other French philosophers, Jefferson conceived of God in terms of matter; and he also argued that God's existence can be known by empirical means. He was influenced in this conception of God to some extent, it seems, by his reading of Priestley and Thomas Cooper, both of whom advanced materialist theologies.[33]

Other fundamental principles that Jefferson examined during his final retirement were in the area of ethics.

Long before the retirement he had made it evident that he assumed a moral sense theory of morality, which proposed that men, in general, naturally possess a faculty whose function is to indicate what they ought to do in their individual moral situations. He had not, however, investigated several key issues pertinent to his theory. He had held that all men have a natural right to pursue happiness, but he had not specified the place of happiness in his moral thought. He had written about moral rules and virtues and had allowed for relativity in ethical judgments, but he made no effort to reconcile these with his moral sense principle. What helped stir him to analyze these issues was his reading of works by the British moralist Thomas Law and the French philosopher Destutt de Tracy. In letters to Law, John Adams, and others, he set forth his conclusions.[34] Happiness is man's well-being or his God-given end. The moral sense indicates what action in a given situation will tend to promote one's well-being as well as that of others. A moral rule is a generalization by reason based on the judgments of the moral sense; and a moral virtue is a habit of action that will enhance the well-being of oneself and other creatures. Because the conditions of happiness in one society may not contribute to happiness in another, the actions that are right in one society may not be right in another. It is not certain what the source of Jefferson's notion of happiness was, but it might have been some of the classic philosophers that he had read. He did not identify happiness with pleasure, which was a widely accepted meaning of the term by eighteenth-century philosophers. By happiness he appears to have meant man's optimal use of his faculties (including the pleasure supervening upon their use) in accordance with natural law, which was a meaning generally compatible with the definition accepted by many classic philosophers. It is evident, however, that his thinking on moral rules and virtues relates to Western society. From the thinking of the stoics, he took prudential rules and virtues whereby a person should act with respect to his own happiness. But it was from the teachings of Jesus, which he had begun to study assiduously by the start of the nineteenth century, that he selected rules and virtues pertinent to human duties, that is, rules and virtues whereby a person should guide his actions toward other persons.[35]

At the same time that Jefferson was reflecting upon his primary philosophical assumptions, he was also occupied with developing plans for public education in Virginia. As already indicated, he had not lost interest in education when he held national office; but he seems to have had few opportunities to conceive practical educational measures. During his second presidential administration, when there was a federal treasury surplus, he did consult with several congressmen on a bill for establishing a national university at Washington and proposed to Congress that it create some academic institutions; but Congress appropriated the treasury surplus to other projects instead. A few years after entering his final retirement, Jefferson, having seen in France the advantages of agricultural education, presented a scheme for the formation of voluntary societies in the various counties of Virginia to promote continuing education in agriculture; but he was unable to arouse substantial support. Several years later, however, he found conditions somewhat favorable to a renewed effort at instituting a public educational system in Virginia.

A number of the leading figures in the state were dissatisfied with the College of William and Mary, which they regarded as too closely tied to the Episcopal Church to serve the public's higher educational needs adequately. And by 1814 they had become sufficiently dissatisfied to lay the groundwork, under Jefferson's leadership, for a private college at Charlottesville, which would soon be supplanted by the University of Virginia. In 1815 the federal government distributed its treasury surplus among the various states. Virginia received about one million dollars and applied the sum to an educational fund; and a commission was appointed, which included Jefferson, to advise on the use of the fund. Working in collaboration with Joseph C. Cabell, Jefferson drafted, in 1817, a bill proposing a system of public education for the state.[36] As far as primary and secondary schooling was concerned, the bill, although it called for a literacy test for citizenship (an idea probably suggested to Jefferson by his reading of the Spanish Constitution of 1812) and for utilitarian (navigation and surveying) as well as liberal studies in the secondary schools, was rather similar to Jefferson's general education bill of 1779. But, with regard to higher education, the bill recommended the establishment of a new university. The legislature rejected the bill, which had been submitted by Cabell; but it did vote some scholarship money for the primary education of poor children.

Despite its negative attitude, the legislature charged the education fund commission to consider specifically the establishment of a university. The commission's report, which was written by Jefferson, presented in 1818, and soon accepted, set forth measures for creating, at Charlottesville, the University of Virginia. It proposed that the university, consisting of various schools, prepare students to be leaders in the public and private sectors of the state and recommended a curriculum stressing languages, philosophy, mathematics, science, and technology, including courses relating to agriculture.[37] Before his death, on July 4, 1826, Jefferson was to see the University of Virginia in operation and to serve as its first rector.

· NOTES ·

1. Cf. Dumas Malone, *Jefferson the Virginian* (Boston: Little, Brown, 1948), Chaps. 1, 2.

2. To John Harvie (January 14, 1760), in Julian P. Boyd *et al.* (eds.), *The Papers of Thomas Jefferson*, 17 vols. published, 50 vols. projected (Princeton, N.J.: Princeton University Press, 1950 et seq.), I, 3.

3. *Autobiography*, in P. L. Ford (ed.), *The Works of Thomas Jefferson*, "Federal Edition," 12 vols. (New York: Putnam, 1904–1905), I, 6.

4. *Ibid.*

5. See Malone, *op. cit.*, Chap. 5.

6. Cf. *The Literary Bible of Thomas Jefferson: His Commonplace Book of Philosophers and Poets*, with an Introduction by Gilbert Chinard (Baltimore: The Johns Hopkins University Press, 1928).

7. To Thomas Law (June 13, 1814), in A. A. Lipscomb and A. E. Bergh (eds.), *The Writings of Thomas Jefferson*, "Memorial Edition," 20 vols. (Washington, D.C.:

Thomas Jefferson Memorial Association, 1903–1904), XIV, 144.

8. To Thomas Turpen (February 5, 1769), in Boyd, *op. cit.*, I, 23–24.

9. Ford, *op. cit.*, I, 470 ff.

10. Cf. Malone, *op. cit.*, Chaps. 11, 12.

11. From Perkins, Buchanan & Brown (October 2, 1769), in Boyd, *op. cit.*, I, 33–34.

12. To John Page (July 15, 1763), in Boyd, *op. cit.*, I, 9–11.

13. To Robert Skipwith (August 3, 1771), in Boyd, *op. cit.*, I, 76–77. Cf. Adrienne Koch, *The Philosophy of Thomas Jefferson* (New York: Columbia University Press, 1943), Chaps. 1–4.

14. *The Commonplace Book of Thomas Jefferson: A Repertory of His Ideas on Government,* with an Introduction and notes by Gilbert Chinard (Baltimore: The Johns Hopkins University Press, 1926), 95–135.

15. "Resolution of the House of Burgesses Designating a Day of Fasting and Prayer," in Boyd, *op. cit.*, I, 105 ff.

16. "Draft of Instructions to the Virginia Delegates in the Continental Congress," in Boyd, *op. cit.*, I, 121 ff.

17. "Jefferson's Fair Copy for the Committee," in Boyd, *op. cit.*, I, 199 ff.

18. "Jefferson's 'original Rough draught' of the Declaration of Independence," in Boyd, *op. cit.*, I, 423 ff.

19. "Third Draft by Jefferson," in Boyd, *op. cit.*, I, 363.

20. To Edmund Pendleton (August 26, 1776), in Boyd, *op. cit.*, I, 504.

21. Cf. Stuart G. Brown, *Thomas Jefferson* (New York: Washigton Square Press, 1963), pp. 208 ff.

22. *Autobiography,* in Ford, *op. cit.*, I, 77–78.

23. "A Bill for the More General Diffusion of Knowledge," in Boyd, *op. cit.*, II, 526 ff.

24. "A Bill for Amending the Constitution of the College of William and Mary, . . . ," in Boyd, *op. cit.*, II, 535 ff.

25. "A Bill for Establishing a Public Library," in Boyd, *op. cit.*, II, 544 ff.

26. *The Commonplace Book of Thomas Jefferson*, Chinard, *op. cit.*, p. 259.

27. *Notes on the State of Virginia* (Queries XIV & XVIII), in Ford, *op. cit.*, IV, 48–59, 82–84.

28. See Dumas Malone, *Jefferson and the Rights of Man* (Boston: Little, Brown, 1951), Chap. 6. Also, see Koch, *op. cit.*, Chaps. 6–9.

29. Cf. "Jefferson's opinion on the Constitutionality of the Residence Bill," in Boyd, *op. cit.*, XVII, 195.

30. Cf. letter to John Tyler (June 28, 1804), in Lipscomb and Bergh, *op. cit.*, XI, 33–34.

31. To Benjamin Rush (April 21, 1803), in Lipscomb and Bergh, *op. cit.*, X, 381–385.

32. To Joseph Priestley (January 27, 1800), in Lipscomb and Bergh, *op. cit.*, X, 146–147.

33. Cf. letter to John Adams (August 15, 1820), in L. J. Cappon (ed.), *The Adams-Jefferson Letters*, 2 vols. (Chapel Hill: The University of North Carolina Press, 1959), II, 567–569.

34. Cf. letter to John Adams (October 14, 1816) in Cappon, *op. cit.*, II, 492.

35. To William Short (October 31, 1819), in Ford, *op. cit.*, XII, 141–142.

36. "A Bill for Establishing a System of Public Education," in Roy J. Honeywell, *The Educational Work of Thomas Jefferson* (Cambridge, Mass.: Harvard University Press, 1931), pp. 233 ff.

37. "Report of the Commissioners Appointed to Fix the Site of the University of Virginia, &c.," in Honeywell, *op. cit.*, pp. 248 ff.

· IV ·
Philosophical Principles of Education

Even though Thomas Jefferson was quite interested in many theoretical aspects of education, he does not appear to have ever attempted to conceive a distinct educational theory. He wrote about education only as it was related to something else, namely, republican society or personal betterment. He never attempted to define the nature of education or even the word "education"; and he never devoted a sustained inquiry into any major educational topics or issues. But Jefferson did formulate philosophical ideas possessing great theoretical significance for education. Although his philosophical views are not completely adequate as principles of education, it is on them that Jefferson's educational proposals are grounded.

I

Jefferson's basic philosophical ideas involve two serious difficulties. As stated by him, they are rather vague and include some inconsistencies. The lack of clarity cannot be overcome, but the inconsistencies may be remedied after a fashion.[1]

For convenience Jefferson's chief philosophical ideas may be divided into two groups, those of methodology and those of nature. The methodological principles are described in a letter to John Adams. (The eccentricities of spelling have been retained.)

> . . . I was obliged to recur ultimately to my habitual anodyne, "I feel: therefore I exist." I feel bodies which are not myself: there are other existences then. I call them matter. I feel them changing place. This gives me motion. Where there is an absence of matter, I call it void, or nothing, or immaterial space. On the basis of sensation, of matter and motion, we may erect the fabric of all the certainties we can have or need. I can concieve thought to be an action of a particular organisation of matter, formed for that purpose by it's creator, as well as that attraction is an action of matter, or magnetism of loadstone. . . . To talk of immaterial existence is to talk of nothings. To say that the human soul, angels, god, are immaterial is to say they are nothings, or that there is no god, no angels, no soul. . . .
>
> Rejecting all organs of information therefore but my senses, I rid myself of the Pyrrhonisms with which an indulgence in speculations hyperphysical and antiphysical so uselessly occupy and disquiet the mind. A single sense may indeed be sometimes decieved, but rarely: and never all our senses together, with their faculty of reasoning.

They evidence realities; and there are enough of these for all the purposes of life, without plunging into the fathomless abyss of dreams and phantasms. I am satisfied, and sufficiently occupied with the things which are, without tormenting or troubling myself about those which may indeed be, but of which I have no evidence.[2]

In the discussion Jefferson is attempting to arrive at principles of the source of knowledge and of the realm of existential subject matter that are appropriate to inquiry. He, consequently, sets forth several criteria that he desires such terms to satisfy. They should yield conclusions supported by evidence, include no inconsistencies, provide explanations of natural phenomena, and take into account the purposes of human life.[3] If Jefferson uses any measure for choosing these criteria, he does not say what it is. He simply takes them as starting points, but does not regard them as truths, or references to any fixed world order.

Jefferson makes clear in the quoted passage that he regards sensory experience, matter, and motion as best satisfying the starting points. Sensory experience is made the source of knowledge, and matter and motion are taken to constitute the universe of existential subject matters. At no place does he mention having "deduced" these three principles from his starting points. He appears, therefore, to accept an empiricist-materialist position only because it is more compatible with the starting points than any other known to him. Consequently, the concepts of sensory experience, matter, and motion are not truths of the world, or references to forms in nature; rather, they signify conventionally selected characteristics of particular sensations, bodies, and motions. Jefferson strongly supports this point in another letter.

> *Nature has, in truth, produced units only through all her works. Classes, orders, genera, species, are not of her work. Her creation is of individuals. . . . This infinitude of units or individuals being far beyond the capacity of our memory, we are obliged, in aid of that, to distribute them into masses, throwing into each of these all the individuals which have a certain degree of resemblance; to sub-divide these into smaller groups. . . . In doing this, we fix arbitrarily on such characteristic resemblances and differences as seem to us most prominent and invariable in the several subjects, and most likely to take a strong hold in our memories.*[4]

In sum, Jefferson has declared himself a nominalist. According to nominalism, any existing thing is a particular; nothing in general—no kind, form, or essence—exists. For instance, this or that dog exists; but canine nature, or "dogness," does not. Because nominalism disallows the existence of universals, it rejects the notion that a general term may refer to something in general which exists. What a general term signifies in existence, nominalism contends, is humanly determined class characteristics, that is, the features whereby a group of particulars are decided by human convention to resemble one another. Thus, the term "dog," rather than referring to some existing canine nature, signifies nothing more than the characteristics whereby men decide, for their convenience, that certain particular things resemble each other—for example, the characteristics of four legs, meat-eating, and barking. Since, for nominalism, the referent of a general term is selected with a view to human convenience, it is not fixed, or permanent; for as human convenience may alter, the referent may change. The philosophical position traditionally opposed to nominalism is metaphysical realism. According to this position, there are things in general—forms or essences—which exist; therefore, a general term may signify something in general which exists. Thus, the term "man" may refer to an existing human nature. For the metaphysical realist, the things in general that exist are what they are independently of any human decision; the referent of a general term may be unalterable. In later discussion, it will be shown that Jefferson's principles of nature follow a metaphysical realist position and, therefore, stand opposed to the nominalism of his methodological principles.

Jefferson's remarks concerning the meanings of his empiricist-materialist terms are suggestive but certainly not very lucid. In discussing the signification of "motion," he stops at saying simply that it means the change of position of a body. Happily, he goes somewhat further in his comments on the meaning of "matter." Besides asserting that matter refers to bodies, he indicates that major corporeal qualities are extension, figure, and mobility. Moreover, he possibly accepted the Lockean position of regarding secondary sense qualities—colors, smells, tastes, sounds, and feelings—as contents of sensations but not as corporeal properties; however, he is mute on this distinction. Jefferson also associates two other traits with matter. Bodies can affect sense organs and cause sensations of themselves; and bodies differ from one another in their functions by virtue of their being organized in diverse ways. For example, thought is an activity of a body organized in one way, and magnetism is an activity of a body organized in another manner. Finally, in accordance with Jefferson's nominalism, which rejects the existence of universals, no general corporeal trait exists. There is only, for example, this length or that shape. More emphatically, no body contains any universal.

Unfortunately, Jefferson is almost silent on what he intends by "sensation." Even so, he appears to attribute to sensations features that are in keeping with the Lockean tradition: the existence of a sensation is ultimately caused by the action of some body upon some sense organ; and, although a sensation may be a perception of matters not existing beyond the sensation, it may also be a perception of matters whose existence is independent of the sensation. For Locke and his followers, sounds, odors, colors, feelings, and flavors depend upon perception for their existence. They, in other words, exist only in the mind and in no way resemble the properties of bodies external to the mind. On the other hand, extension, figure, motion, and solidity are properties of external bodies as well as contents of perceptions. So, a sensation of heat, even when it is directly caused by a body acting upon the senses, does not represent any property of the body. But a sensation of motion may represent a property of a body acting upon the senses.

Even though Jefferson's examination of his basic methodological principles is superficial, it does adumbrate a doctrine of existential meaning and one of existential truth. Bodies are existences; and immaterial things, because the absence of matter is void, are nothing. Any term or statement, consequently, can refer to a thing of existence only if it has a material content. Hence, the terms and propositions of pure mathematics, being conventional abstractions from experience of corporeal matters but with no reference to them, have no existential import.[5] And, as Jefferson affirms above, even a conception of God, angel, or soul must intend an object with some sort of material aspect before it can be significant of something in existence. All that one can know of material objects comes through the senses. To say, accordingly, that a term or statement must have a material content is to say that it has to be somehow expressible in sensory terms. A perception is true of a given existing object if it corresponds with that object, and the perception may be taken as corresponding with the object if it is found to cohere with all other perceptions relevant to the object: "A single sense may indeed be sometimes decieved, but rarely; and never all our senses together." [6] Similarly, a conception about things in existence may be taken as true if it coheres with the facts, or true perceptions, pertinent to the things: "A patient pursuit of facts, and cautious combination and comparison of them, is the drudgery to which man is subjected by his Maker, if he wishes to attain sure knowledge." [7] In keeping with Jefferson's nominalism, which denies the existence of universals beyond the mind, the contents of conceptions, being universals, cannot be said to correspond with anything in existence apart from the mind.

Jefferson's chief principles of nature are indicated in a letter to John Adams showing his rejection of both orthodox Christianity and the atheism held by some French philosophers:

On the contrary I hold (without appeal to revelation) that when we take a view of the Universe, in it's parts general or particular, it is impossible for the human mind not to percieve and feel a conviction of design, consummate skill, and indefinite power in every atom of it's composition. The movements of the heavenly bodies, so exactly held in their course by the balance of centrifugal and centripetal forces, the structure of our earth itself, with it's distribution of lands, waters and atmosphere, animal and vegetable bodies, examined in all their minutest particles, insects mere atoms of life, yet as perfectly organized as man or mammoth, the mineral substances, their generation and uses, it is impossible, I say, for the human mind not to believe that there is, in all this, design, cause and effect, up to an ultimate cause, a fabricator of all things from matter and motion, their preserver and regulator while permitted to exist in their present forms, and their regenerator into new and other forms. We see, too, evident proofs of the necessity of a superintending power to maintain the Universe in it's course and order. Stars, well known, have disappeared, new ones have come into view, comets, in their incalculable courses, may run foul of suns and planets and require renovation under other laws; certain races of animals are become extinct; and, were there no restoring power, all existences might extinguish successively, one by one, until all should be reduced to a shapeless chaos. So irresistible are these evidences of an intelligent and powerful Agent that, of the infinite numbers of men who have existed thro' all time, they have believed, in the proportion of a million at least to Unit, in the hypothesis of an eternal pre-existence of a creator, rather than in that of a self-existent Universe.[8]

During the course of this argument, Jefferson explains nature in three major terms: God, natural creature, and natural order.

As the passage reveals, the existence and nature of

God are approached by Jefferson more or less from his sensationalist-materialist position as already described. He seeks knowledge of the existence and nature of God not from revelation (or on a priori grounds) but through observation of the universe. Seeing a world of design, order, and preservation, he concludes that there must be a deity, namely, the creator, regulator, and restorer of the world. And he maintains, elsewhere, that his conclusion, at least with respect to God's existence, is acceptable to anyone who inspects the universe with an open mind; for Jefferson holds that the structure of the world makes God's existence as obvious to the senses as walking across a room makes manifest the existence of motion.[9] That God's existence is quite apparent is testified to, Jefferson asserts above, by the common opinion of mankind, which affirms the divine existence. Viewing God as the fabricator, regulator, and restorer of a material world and adamantly arguing that an immaterial cannot act upon a material substance, Jefferson thinks, presumably, that the deity must be material in some mode. But in what mode he never bothers to explain. Regardless of his materialistic notion of God, Jefferson attributes to the deity some traits traditionally regarded as divine, namely, omniscience, omnipotence, and omnibenevolence.[10] He clarifies the traits very little, however. For example, it may be pointed out that, although Jefferson's conception of God is helpful in accounting for any order and goodness in the world, it does not appear to explain any disjointedness and evil that exist: one would think that there could not be disorder and evil in a creation by an infinitely intelligent, potent, and benevolent being.

Despite the apparent agreement of Jefferson's discussion on God's existence and nature with his sensationalist-materialist position as previously described, the argument does seem to depart from a salient feature of his methodology. The methodology, it will be recalled, does not appear to refer to any set structure or order in the universe; in fact, because it comprehends a nominalism, it seems to spurn such a structure and order. The argument of God's existence and nature, however, appeals to a fixed organization of the world. One is told that there is "design, consummate skill, and indefinite power in every atom" of the universe's composition. Furthermore, one is not left to think that this organization is to be explained by the way that people look at the world; rather, one is told that it is to be explained by an actual deity (as opposed to a conception of God employed merely as a methodological principle), who has created and who regulates and restores the universe according to his plan. In other words, the discourse on God's existence and nature, quite unlike the methodology, lays claim to truths of the world.

According to Jefferson, natural creatures have two main features in common other than the fact that they are all material. The end to which God has created the universe is not discernible; it is beyond the grasp of human intellect, which is finite. Nevertheless, it is evident that the deity has assigned his creatures and their parts, whether mineral, vegetable, or animal, definite ends. Thus, Jefferson sides with the "Theist [who urges] . . . the palpable existence of final causes, that the eye was made to see, and the ear to hear, and not that we see because we have eyes, and hear because we have ears." [11] In brief, Jefferson adheres, on empirical grounds, to a doctrine of final causes in nature. In addition to final causes,

God has endowed his creatures with forms, or natures. This point is obviously presumed by Jefferson in his discussions of human faculties. For instance, he writes that man's moral sense "is as much a part of his nature as the sense of hearing, seeing, feeling." [12] But, regardless of his use of an idea of natural forms, Jefferson gives it little explication. Jefferson's ascription of forms and final causes to nature is, of course, a part of his viewing the world as having a fixed structure and order. It is almost needless to say that the attribution of forms and final causes to nature, apparently involving a metaphysical realism of sorts, stands in flat contradiction to the nominalistic aspect of his methodology. It most significantly opposes that feature with regard to the nature of bodies and of sensations. According to Jefferson's nominalism, no body contains universals or, therefore, an essence. According to his idea of natural creatures, however, bodies do have forms. In view of his nominalism, perceptions can never comprehend a universal; thus, the contents of conceptions are not to be found in existence apart from the mind. But with respect to his idea of natural creatures, perceptions, if they are to apprize one of the forms in nature, must be able to apprehend universals; hence, the contents of conceptions may exist independently of the mind. Because Jefferson's imputation of forms and final causes to nature opposes the nominalistic aspect of his methodology regarding the nature of bodies and sensations, it also contradicts that aspect on existential truth. To say that a conception is true of existential objects is simply to hold, in view of his nominalism, that the conception coheres with the facts, or true perceptions, relevant to itself. However, in accordance with his idea of natural creatures, to say that a conception is true of existential objects is also to contend that it corresponds with something existing in nature, namely, a universal. Jefferson most obviously employs his realistic doctrine of truth in his moral and political writings, as in the Declaration of Independence: "We hold these truths to be sacred & undeniable; that all men are created equal & independant: that from that equal creation they derive rights inherent & inalienable." [13]

The order of nature, which for Jefferson is ascertainable through sensory experience and holds for the movements and actions of material creatures, includes, first of all, the divine plan of creation. Pertaining to all creatures in the universe, the plan is the most general law of nature. Second, the order of nature contains physical laws, which consist of the sorts of movements that creatures tend to follow regardless of any choice on their part. In other words, physical laws relate to creatures insofar as they are not free, or self-governing. Third, the order of nature involves moral laws, which pertain to creatures that are free, or self-governing. These laws prescribe the kinds of actions that free creatures should follow when they are in positions of moral agents. One hardly needs to be told that this notion of natural order is incompatible with the nominalism of Jefferson's methodology, which would seem to deny any fixed structures in the universe and would appear to take physical and moral laws merely to be human formulations for human purposes.

Jefferson's educational inquiries, which are largely concerned with the educational problems of political democracy, are guided by his ideas of sensation, matter, and motion as well as those of God, natural creature, and natural order. But the inquiries are led by these concepts only insofar as the latter are conceivable from the standpoint of his realism. His nominalism is not ingredient to the philosophical framework of his educational thought. On first glance, his educational investigations might lead one to think that they rest on nominalistic principles. In stressing that men have individual differences, the investigations remind one of the nominalistic belief that the only things which exist are particulars. By contending that the given customs and circumstances of a society must be taken into account by its educators,[14] they suggest that societies differ from one another and, thus, call to mind again the nominalistic belief that only particulars exist. However, a closer look at Jefferson's educational inquiries reveals that they depend upon metaphysical realist principles. In the inquiries Jefferson holds that there is a human nature (constituted by man's psychical faculties)[15] and that individual human differences are explainable not by an absence of human nature but by the point that the essential faculties of various persons possess different degrees of power. He also maintains that there are natural laws and rights (to be *discovered*, not *determined*, by men) which are pertinent to all societies. So, by including Jefferson's basic terms only as they are to be understood with respect to his realism, the philosophical foundation of his educational thought avoids the gross contradictions that arise whenever the empiricist-materialist terms are viewed from both his realism and nominalism.

It should not be concluded, however, that the philosophical framework of Jefferson's educational investigations is free from difficulty. Several of its fundamental philosophical terms are vague: sensation, matter, God, and natural creature—all are more or less obscure in meaning.

II

Jefferson's principles of human nature, morality, and political society are also integral to his philosophical orientation to education. Unfortunately, these principles cannot be wholly understood because they depend for their meanings, in part, upon Jefferson's metaphysical ideas, which, as already observed, are sometimes obscure. And, even when considered apart from the metaphysical ideas, the principles have areas of vagueness. Nevertheless, a survey of them can be helpful in inspecting Jefferson's educational proposals.

According to Jefferson, man, being a divine creature, possesses a nature given to him by God. This nature is constituted of various psychical faculties, each of which resides in a corporeal organ and has a divinely assigned end. Reason, by comparing perceptions, conceptions, and proposals with respect to their coherency, determines what is true and contrives courses of action. The moral sense, in view of appropriate information presented to it by reason, discriminates between right and wrong in moral matters. Taste, also dependent upon reason for information, distinguishes between what is beautiful and what is ugly. And the appetites provoke men to care for their biological needs. Other powers, such as memory and imagination as well as the five senses, serve as auxiliaries to these faculties.[16] For some mysterious reason pertaining to his plan of the universe, God has failed to endow relatively few human beings with all of the human faculties. Thus, some men, being exceptions to the general condition of mankind, are born without moral powers. When a certain faculty is absent from a person, the deficiency may be made up, to an extent, by ersatz, or substitute, measures. For example, an idiot may be looked after by a guardian; and a person without a moral sense may be trained in habits of right action.[17] Moreover, many faculties are given to individual men in undeveloped states and in greater or lesser degrees. Thus, an individual's reason, moral sense, taste, memory, and imagination are extremely weak at his birth; and they may be capable of a greater or lesser development than the faculties of another individual.[18] Finally, God does not seem to have placed a fixed limit on the extent of development of human faculties in general. Accordingly, there may be historical progress in the development of human faculties; that is, there may be development of human powers from one historical era to another. Such progress is made possible by man's encountering new circumstances, his profiting from past mistakes and accomplishments, and his accumulation of knowledge.[19]

Jefferson attributes to man a divinely assigned end. He offers no close examination of this end, but he does at least suggest what it is. When men develop their powers as much as possible and employ them fully with respect to their divinely given ends, they are able to conduct investigations concerning truth, to act rightly in practical affairs, and to make and enjoy aesthetic objects. Inasmuch as they are competent in areas of reason, morals, and aesthetics and find pleasure in the exercise of their faculties, they obtain happiness. This, as far as Jefferson is concerned, is

man's well-being, or God-given end. An action which pro-
motes one's happiness or that of another is right: but,
since the circumstances contributing to happiness in one
situation—the included environment and the state of development of the involved persons' faculties—may not be
circumstances creating happiness in another, an action
that is right in one situation may not be right in another.
Consequently, Jefferson allows for some relativity in morality.[20] Because of their individual natural differences, not
all human beings can attain the same portion of happiness. A man with superior faculties can achieve a greater
happiness than that which is possible for a man of lesser
powers. And a man who is lacking the faculty of reason
does not seem capable of any happiness. Regrettably,
Jefferson does not adequately explain why God has not
made all men equally capable of happiness. At best, he
dismisses this difficulty by appealing to the mysteriousness
of the divine plan of creation.

Jefferson points out that man is able to make choices
by virtue of some of his psychical powers. He can choose,
for instance, according to the dictates of his moral sense,
taste, or appetites; and to the extent that man is able to
make choices, he is self-governing. He may or may not be
the only free creature in the universe; but, being self-
governing, he is subject to the moral laws of nature, for
instance, self-preservation, liberty of thought, and the
pursuit of happiness. By acting in accordance with these
laws, man can attain his well-being; otherwise, he cannot.
Through his reason and moral sense a person can acquire
knowledge of moral natural laws. To live by such laws,
however, he need not know what they are; he has only to
follow his moral sense. Moral laws of nature apply to a

person whenever he is in the position of a moral agent, namely, whenever he is in a situation in which the well-being of some creature, human or not, is at stake and he is able to choose a course of action affecting that well-being. Through his reason he can learn of the facts pertinent to the situation and propose alternatives of action; and, in view of these facts and alternatives, he can judge, through his moral sense, which available course of action is right. The alternative judged as right by the moral sense concords with the moral natural laws.[21] Needless to say, men do not always act as they should. For Jefferson, man's immoral acts stem from his appetites and passions, which, when intense, interfere with the workings of reason and the moral sense.

Because God has intended that human beings, generally speaking, are to attain their well-being, he has given them the rights to all conditions, objects, and actions necessary for attaining it. To put the case in Jefferson's familiar phrasing: "We hold these truths to be sacred & undeniable; that all men are created equal & independant; that from that equal creation they derive rights inherent & inalienable, among which are the preservation of life, & liberty, & the pursuit of happiness." [22] Because the conditions, objects, and actions necessary for happiness in one situation may not be necessary for happiness in another situation, the members of one situation may recognize natural rights that are not recognized by the members of another situation. Inasmuch as God has endowed human beings with faculties whereby to achieve their well-being, he has given them the right to an optimal development of these faculties. Also, a person born without some faculty has a right to whatever measures, if any, can rectify the deficiency. Because no person can develop his faculties beyond their fixed limits, he does not have a right to objects, conditions, and actions tending to develop faculties beyond those limits; and he does not have a right to participate in activities that demand the capabilities of faculties stronger than his.

Since men, because of their appetites and passions, do not always act toward one another as they should, they do not, by their nature, necessarily respect one another's natural rights. Thus, in a state of nature, that is, in a condition where men govern themselves by nothing more than their individual appetites and decisions, they may very well prevent one another from exercising their natural rights and, thereby, from achieving their well-being. Human beings, consequently, must not live in a state of nature; they must enter political society, whose legitimate purpose, for Jefferson, is to protect its members' natural rights and promote their happiness. According to Jefferson, there are three major types of political society.[23] One is tyranny, wherein the rulers, governing mainly by physical coercion, seek their own interests regardless of the public will, which is the opinion of the majority of the public. Jefferson looked upon the England of George III and Napoleonic France as tyrannies. A second type of political society is the informal republic, wherein the public will rules—not through formal government but through custom and popular opinion. In Jefferson's opinion, the North American Indians lived in informal republics. Finally, there is the formal republic, wherein the public will rules through formal government. It was this kind of society which Jefferson wanted the United States to be. Any tyranny, for Jefferson, is a corrupt political society. Because its rulers disregard the public will, they violate the natural right of self-government and, in so doing, act counter to political society's legitimate aim of protecting the public's natural rights. Whereas an informal republic is capable of securing its public's natural rights, it is appropriate to small societies only, which can be organized without formal government. On the other hand, a formal democracy, which is also suitable for protecting its public's natural rights, is relevant to large societies. It is the formal republic with which Jefferson, who lived in a comparatively large society, was primarily concerned.

There are conditions that Jefferson contends must be satisfied if a large society is to be a workable formal republic. (1) The society's constitution must not only outline the structure and powers of government and specify the public's natural rights but must also be amendable and subject to the approval of each new generation of the society's members. Through amendment and generation-to-generation approval, the constitution can be made to reflect major changes within the public's will, which are likely to arise from alterations in historical circumstances. (2) To assure that its officials will be responsive to its will, the society's public must elect them, hold them to comparatively short terms of office, and scrutinize them. (3) The administration of public affairs pertaining to the society as a whole must belong to an agency governing the society as a whole; but the administration of public affairs special to some part of the society—say, a region, county, or ward—must belong to a governmental agency of that part. In this way, regional and local circumstances can be given special consideration. (4) The society's laws must concord with moral natural laws and not violate natural rights. (5) The majority of the society's members must respect the minority's natural rights. Otherwise, the society's government, in following the public will, is quite likely to ignore or infringe upon the minority's natural rights. (6) In order to gain information pertaining to threats to and opportunities for the exercise of its natural rights, the society's public must have access to free media of mass communication. (7) To help assure that its citizens will be prepared to perform the many tasks necessary to its operation, the society must furnish them an appropriate education. More specifically, education in the society must prepare some citizens to be leaders, enable all citizens to exercise the ordinary rights of self-government, and ready all citizens for the pursuit of happiness.

· NOTES ·

1. Section I of this chapter is contained, with some differences, in a previously published article by the author. See Robert D. Heslep, "Thomas Jefferson's Major Philosophical Principles," *Educational Theory,* XVI (April 1966), 152–161.
2. To John Adams (August 15, 1820), in L. J. Cappon (ed.), *The Adams-Jefferson Letters,* 2 vols. (Chapel Hill: The University of North Carolina Press, 1959), II, 567–569.
3. Elsewhere, Jefferson suggests logical economy as a criterion. Cf. letter to John Adams (March 14, 1820), in Cappon, *op. cit.,* II, 562.
4. To Dr. John Manners (February 22, 1814), in A. A.

Lipscomb and A. E. Bergh (eds.), *The Writings of Thomas Jefferson,* "Memorial Edition," 20 vols. (Washington, D.C.: Thomas Jefferson Memorial Association, 1903–1904), XIV, 97–98.

5. Cf. letter to Dr. Benjamin Rush (August 17, 1811), in Lipscomb and Bergh, *op. cit.,* XIII, 75.

6. Cappon, *loc. cit.*

7. *Notes on the State of Virginia* (Query VI), in P. L. Ford (ed.), *The Works of Thomas Jefferson,* "Federal Edition," 12 vols. (New York: Putnam, 1904–1905), III, 462n.

8. To John Adams (April 11, 1823), in Cappon, *op. cit.,* II, 592.

9. To John Adams (April 8, 1816), in Cappon, *op. cit.,* II, 467–468.

10. To John Adams (April 11, 1823), in Cappon, *op. cit.,* II, 591 *et ad passim.*

11. To John Adams (April 8, 1816), in Lipscomb and Bergh, *op. cit.,* XIV, 469.

12. To Peter Carr (August 10, 1787), in Julian P. Boyd *et al.* (eds.), *The Papers of Thomas Jefferson,* 17 vols. published, 50 vols. projected (Princeton, N.J.: Princeton University Press, 1950 et seq.), XII, 15.

13. "Jefferson's 'original Rough draught' of the Declaration of Independence," in Boyd, *op. cit.,* I, 424.

14. Cf. letter to John Bannister (October 15, 1785), in Boyd, *op. cit.,* VIII, 636–637.

15. Cf. "Report of the Commissioners Appointed to Fix the Site of the University of Virginia, &c.," in Roy J. Honeywell, *The Educational Work of Thomas Jefferson* (Cambridge, Mass.: Harvard University Press, 1931), 248 ff.

16. Cf. letter to Thomas Law (June 13, 1814), in Lipscomb and Bergh, *op. cit.,* XIV, 138–143.

17. *Ibid.,* p. 142.

18. Cf. letter to Peter Carr (August 10, 1787), in Boyd, *op. cit.,* XII, 14–15.

19. Cf. letter to Samuel Kercheval (July 12, 1816), in Ford, *op. cit.,* XII, 11–12.

20. Cf. letter to John Adams (October 14, 1816), in Cappon, *op. cit.*, II, 492.

21. "Opinion on the question whether the United States have a right to renounce their treaties with France, . . . ," in Lipscomb and Bergh, *op. cit.*, III, 228.

22. "Jefferson's 'original Rough draught' of the Declaration of Independence," in Boyd, *op. cit.*, I, 424.

23. Cf. letter to James Madison (January 30, 1787), in Boyd, *op. cit.*, XI, 92–93.

· V ·
Educational Proposals

Thomas Jefferson's educational proposals were of two kinds, theoretical and practical. The former were intended by him to have universal significance, whereas the latter were meant to be relevant mainly to particular situations. The theoretical proposals guided Jefferson in his formulation of the practical ones, and the theoretical ones were conceived within the framework of his philosophical principles.

I

Jefferson's theoretical proposals are mostly devoted to several key topics of education, and one means of comprehending many of the proposals as they reflect his philosophical principles is to examine the topics from the standpoint of the principles. In such an investigation, one can observe that the principles present difficulties related especially to education—vaguenesses concerning educational purpose, method, and administration.

One topic with which the theoretical proposals are concerned is educational purpose. Unfortunately, the proposals do not make possible a full understanding of the topic; most conspicuously, they do not clarify the defining characteristics of an educational purpose. At their best, they indicate a conception of education's purpose for formal republican society.

According to Jefferson's philosophical principles, the end of any republican society, whether formal or informal, is the maintenance of the natural rights of the society's members. This entails that the society will help assure the optimal development of each member's faculties with respect to his happiness and otherwise make feasible each member's exercise of his rights to the actions, objects, and conditions necessary for his happiness. More specifically, a formal republic must have a public that is prepared to undertake self-government; and the purpose of education for formal republican society may be generally viewed as threefold: to prepare some citizens to be public leaders, to enable all citizens to exercise the common rights of self-government, and to ready all citizens for the pursuit of happiness in the society's private sphere.

Although education's purpose for one formal republic will be generally the same as it is for any other, it need not be completely the same; for the purpose as it relates to a given formal republic is determined in part by that society's special circumstances. Because of differing circumstances, some actions, conditions, and objects necessary for happiness in one formal republic may not be required in another; therefore there may be natural rights pertinent to one formal republic that will not be relevant to another. And, also because of varying circumstances, the private pursuits of happiness available to the members of one formal republic might not be present to those of another. Accordingly, education in one formal republic may not need to apprize students of natural rights which education in another should inform them; and education in one formal republic might not need to prepare students for some private pursuits of happiness which education in another should ready them. For example, circumstances were such in small ancient democracies that mass media of communication were not required; therefore it was not necessary to inform students of this right, whereas education in modern democracies, which must have free mass media of communications, should acquaint students with this key right. Similarly, education in ancient democracies was not obligated to ready students for many of the vocations that education in modern republics is obligated to provide for them.

Although the educational objective for a given formal republic, according to Jefferson, must be conceived in view of that society's special circumstances, the purpose must also be formulated to relate to the natural differences among the students of that society. Three reasons support this point. (1) A republic needs leaders, in its private as well as its public sectors, who are especially talented and virtuous; and the only people who are capable of being such leaders are those who are natural aristocrats, namely, those who possess extraordinarily strong powers of reason, morals, and taste. Therefore, education in a republic must aim to locate those students who are natural aristocrats and prepare them to be leaders. (2) Similarly, a republic requires ordinary workers in its private and public spheres; and they do not need to be people with extraordinarily strong faculties. Thus, education in such a society should aim to identify those students with lesser faculties and enable them to assume the society's ordinary tasks. (3) Because God has given man faculties to attain his well-being, he has given him the right to fully develop his faculties to that end. Thus, education in a republic should aim to develop each student's faculties fully with respect to his happiness. It follows, incidentally, that not all students in a republic are entitled to the same educational opportunities; for each student has a right to only those that are commensurate with the strength of his faculties. As Jefferson wrote of Virginia, "it is the duty of its functionaries, to provide that every citizen in it should receive an education *proportioned to the condition and pursuits of his life.*" [1]

Subject matter, or that which is to be studied, is another educational topic with which Jefferson's theoretical proposals are concerned. Although the proposals deal with the topic mostly as it relates to education in a democracy, they treat it in a fairly comprehensive way. In examining the topic, one will do well to start with a consideration of Jefferson's principles of existence.

Jefferson holds that whatever exists is material and only material in some fashion, and he allows that forms as well as particulars may exist. Forms, however, do not exist apart from particulars except in thought. One existent is God. Other existents, those of nature, are created by God; still others are made by man. Among natural existents, which have forms, there are minerals, plants, and animals; and there are natural laws. Of man-made existents, which may have forms, two types are quite familiar. One kind consists of those that serve as means to ends, for example, weapons, language, and political society. The other sort comprizes existents that are made for their own sakes, notably, aesthetic objects. God, natural existents, and man-made existents are tantamount to the universe of subject matters of education.

Men have facts and generalizations as knowledge of existents. Factual knowledge is knowledge of an existent as nothing more than a particular; and general knowledge is knowledge of existents as members of a group. General knowledge may be knowledge of a form that is shared by the members of a group, knowledge of a law followed by the members, or just knowledge of what is probably true of them or what is true of them for the most part. Factual knowledge is obtained directly through the senses guided by reason; and general knowledge is established by reason, which can make abstractions and determine relations, through an examination of facts. Different disciplines have diverse subject matters. For instance, the subject matter of physics is bodies and their motions; biology is concerned with live natural creatures; history is about events; ethics deals with human actions; and mathematics studies certain abstract forms and the relations among them. Physics, biology, history, and other disciplines purporting to give knowledge relevant to sensory subject matters must employ cognitive methods that are basically, but not necessarily exclusively, empirical. On the other hand, mathematics, whose subject matters have been abstracted by reason from sensory experience and are treated without reference to it, may utilize a strictly rational method. Because of the possible historical progress in the development of human faculties, there may be an advancement of the disciplines from one era to another.[2] Consequently, the teaching of the disciplines is liable to periodic revisions.

By itself no subject matter is more or less real than any other. Jefferson contends that only the material is real; and even though matter appears in various modes, it admits to no gradations. Therefore, there are no degrees of reality. It must not be thought, then, that forms have a higher order of reality than that possessed by particulars or that forms constitute a realm of subject matter inherently superior to that consisting of particulars. Furthermore, no discipline is inherently higher or lower than any other. As just explained, the subject matter of one discipline is as real as that of any other. And, although the knowledge discovered by the empirical disciplines does not have the certainty attached to that reached by mathematics and other rational disciplines, the latter knowledge is irrelevant to the purposes of the empirical disciplines except as a possible tool.

Despite the fact that all subject matters are equally real and that none is inherently higher or lower than another, the disciplines involved in their study may vary in importance from one society to another. With respect to man, subject matters are important to the extent that investigations of them provide knowledge contributive to the attainment of happiness; and some subject matters may yield knowledge that can contribute more to the achievement of happiness than the knowledge had from other subject matters can contribute. Which subject mat-

ters are more important than others in this regard cannot
be absolutely determined, however; for the knowledge
which is able to contribute to the achievement of happiness in one society may not be able to contribute as much
toward that end in another society as some other knowledge might be able to contribute. So, it may be argued,
the teaching of the natural sciences was much more significant for man's well-being in democratic societies during Jefferson's day than it had been in Periclean Athens.
Also, one might wish to add, the study of the classic languages is presently less important for man's well-being in
democracies than it was during Jefferson's time.

Jefferson's theoretical proposals also involve the subject of method, which pertains to any systematic way
whereby educational objectives may be pursued. Although
Jefferson's philosophical principles are not without significance for this topic, they are too vague to specify an educational method. They do not even raise the question of
which method or methods are appropriate to education in
a democracy; but they do intimate practices that are dis-
tinctly methodological in quality and appropriate to education which aims at the student's well-being.

In order to be happy, Jefferson maintains, a human
being must be competent in the areas of reason, morals,
and aesthetics; and, in order to be competent in these
areas, he must be able to use his judgmental faculties—
reason, moral sense, and taste—and their auxiliary powers
—imagination, memory, and the five senses—in view of
their respective natural ends. But at birth, Jefferson allows,
the judgmental faculties and some of their auxiliaries are
too feeble to function. Therefore, if education aims at the
student's well-being, it must develop his natally weak

powers toward their individual natural ends. How this can be done is not readily evident. On the one hand, Jefferson says, these faculties can become stronger only through exercise; but, on the other hand, they are too infirm to attain their ends. Hence, how can a student be made to use his natally weak powers? The answer to this question consists partly of measures comprizing imitation and drill.[3]

Although a person's judgmental faculties and their auxiliaries are too feeble to function at birth, they will, normally, be able to function in a fashion after some physical growth. A child does remember and imagine some things even if he does not do so in view of serving his judgmental powers. And, although he is not able to make cognitive, moral, and aesthetic judgments, he is able to imitate such judgments, whether they are valid or not. Thus, children frequently regard as true, right, and beautiful what their parents deem as such. By repeated and increasingly varied remembering and imagining, a child's powers of memory and imagination become stronger; and, by repeated imitations of increasingly varied cognitive, moral, and aesthetic judgments, a child's reason, moral sense, and taste become gradually stronger and more nearly able to initiate judgments. Because a child will be directed toward making correct judgments only insofar as he has imitated correct ones, he should, in order to strengthen his judgmental powers toward their respective natural ends, imitate only valid judgments. These observations suggest certain kinds of methodological practices relevant to the development of very young students' judgmental powers and their auxiliaries: students should be presented with correct cognitive, moral, and aesthetic judgments and should be led to make recitations of these judgments. The observations also imply that students should be provided with opportunities for "memory work" and imagination. Other measures are apparent, too. To help assure that very young students will be disposed to imitate the judgments presented to them and to do the memorizing and imagining expected of them, the judgments and the memory and imagination projects ought to be placed within contexts that are pleasant to the students. Thus, Jefferson regarded fictional literature as a potentially useful source of moral instruction. To take advantage of any previous development of the students' faculties, a teacher should begin a course of study by presenting judgments for imitation and memory and imagination projects that are relevant to the students' prior experiences. And, because the powers of memory and imagination are auxiliaries to the judgmental faculties, the teacher will do well to make the projects for exercising the former powers relevant to the judgments to be imitated.

After a period of imitation and drill, a student will be somewhat prepared to initiate valid judgments; but he will certainly not be sufficiently ready. His store of information will be slight; and his reason will not have been seriously exercised in determining relations of coherency, in generalizing, and in applying generalizations to concrete situations; thus, his reason will not have been adequately trained to establish facts and general truths. And, to the extent that his reason will not be able to judge what is true, it will not be able to provide his moral and aesthetic powers the knowledge they will need for making sound judgments. Several practices appear to be suitable for eliminating these deficiencies. When the student begins to make judgments, he will increase his store of information; but he may also obtain additional information that he may need in learning to initiate judgments by imitation and drill. To help the student learn to make judgments of factual significance, the teacher should furnish him opportunities for sensory experience of the related subject matters. Field trips and laboratories can be especially appropriate in this regard. In aiding the student to detect relations of coherency, the teacher may begin by pointing out to him coherent relationships that hold within the information which he already possesses. Subsequently, he should direct the student to compare new perceptions and conceptualizations with this information for coherency, which presupposes that the student ought to be guided toward perceptions and conceptualizations whose connections with that information are not obscure to him. To facilitate the student's learning to generalize and to apply generalizations, the teacher may provide models of these procedures. And to help assure that the student learns to make moral and aesthetic judgments in view of relevant knowledge, the teacher should place an emphasis, in moral and aesthetic instruction, upon an examination of the facts and general knowledge pertinent to the given subject matter.

Finally, Jefferson's theoretical views of education include proposals for the administrative organization of education. But because Jefferson was interested in this topic mainly as it pertained to formal republican society, he developed a rather limited theoretical idea of it. Jefferson, it may be remembered, argued that governmental administration in formal republican society should be decentralized. Because a formal republic would be comparatively large, he assumed that such a society would encompass a great number of circumstances relevant to its members' natural rights and that many of these circumstances would be mainly regional or local in scope. Moreover, he maintained that regional or local circumstances could be cared for better by regional and local governmental bodies than by a central government. He concluded, then, that the administrative structure of education in formal republican society ought to be decentralized. Those aspects of education in a formal republic that are mainly local and regional in relevance should be administered respectively by local and regional agencies. The other aspects ought to be administered centrally.

II

Thomas Jefferson's chief practical educational proposals were mostly, as already indicated, his plans for education in Virginia. The general education bills of 1779 and 1817, which he proposed, called for a system of elementary, secondary, and university education and made provisions for the free education of impoverished students. The education fund commission's report of 1818 led to the founding of the University of Virginia. There was the bill for reorganizing the College of William and Mary and the one for establishing a public library (to serve the "learned and curious"). And there was his scheme for instituting agricultural societies. Among his relatively few proposals relating to education in other areas than Virginia, there was the project for a national university; and a notion was entertained concerning the establishment of a national philosophical academy, an institution to be devoted to scholarly and scientific research.[4] Jefferson made his practical educational proposals with guidance from his theoretical ones, but he formulated the proposals also in view of Virginia's and the nation's circumstances.

According to Jefferson's philosophical principles, it will be recalled, the objective of education in a formal republic is to prepare those citizens who are natural aristocrats to be public leaders, to ready all citizens to carry on the common activities of self-government, and to enable them all to pursue happiness as private persons. That Jefferson followed this conception of educational purpose when he drew up his practical educational proposals seems evident. In the general education bill of 1779 he spoke plainly of Virginia's need to prepare gifted students to be public leaders and to train all students for the ordinary affairs of self-government. And in the education fund commission's report of 1818 he made clear also that the state's schools must help ready all students to undertake their private pursuits of happiness. Apparently, Jefferson meant that the bill for a public library was to foster research among Virginia's scholars and scientists, whose increase in knowledge would generally promote the well-being of the state's members. And the idea of a philosophical academy was clearly intended to have a similar end on a national scale. In proposing the county agricultural societies, Jefferson obviously had in mind the immediate objective of furthering the private person's economic well-being, especially the prosperity of individual farmers.

Jefferson was very well informed of the circumstances of Virginia and the United States during his time; and, in following his theoretical view of the aim of education in formal republican society when he framed his practical educational proposals, he was quite attentive to these circumstances. Being a public leader of Virginia entailed being a governor, a state legislator, a state judge, or a member of the United States Congress. But being a public leader involved knowledge and virtues also: a sound understanding of the laws and legal institutions of Virginia and the United States; a cognizance of the objects, actions, and conditions affecting the natural rights of the state's citizens; a strong sense of duty to protect these rights; the ability to gain the confidence of the citizenry; and the capacity to conceive and get enacted measures favorable to the natural rights of the citizens. Virginia required, especially, legislation favorable to various professions that could notably contribute to the well-being of the state's members. Professions in trade and agriculture were obviously important to Virginia's economy. Lawyers and physicians were required by the state's legal and medical problems. Natural scientists were necessary for technological improvements in trade and agriculture, and scholarship was required to determine and preserve the state's heritage. Architects were needed for Virginia's civil and military construction, and professions in the fine arts were necessary to enrich the state's meager aesthetic life. In order to participate properly in the ordinary affairs of self-government in Virginia, the state's citizens had to be informed of their natural rights and the issues pertaining to them; and they had to be disposed to judge the given candidates for office with regard to their relevant qualifications and to scrutinize public officials in view of their care for the public welfare. And, to be able to pursue happiness as private persons, Virginia's citizens had to be qualified for the available vocations as well as inclined to look after their domestic affairs and their leisure in a suitable manner. Jefferson did not think that formal educational institutions could prepare Virginia's students completely with respect to these circumstances; however, he did hold that they should aim at readying them to a considerable extent. More specifically, education in the state must aim at an optimal development of each student's faculties as related to these circumstances.[5]

It was with reference to this formulation of education's purpose in Virginia that Jefferson conceived the courses of study that he recommended for the state. He regarded three academic studies as requisite for all students in Virginia—arithmetic, history, and geography.[6] Arithmetic was looked upon as appropriate for the early strengthening of the rational faculty and helpful in everyday affairs as well as basic to other branches of mathematics. History was not only important as a record of human events but was also viewed as suitable for instruction in Virginia's and the nation's laws, governmental institutions, and civil duties and rights. And geography was perceived as necessary for furnishing students with an understanding of the land in which they lived. Because Jefferson wanted all Virginia's students to have these three studies, he stipulated that arithmetic, history, and geography be offered during the first three years of schooling, when all students in the state would have some financial means (public or private) to attend school. To be sure, he thought that the reading and writing of English and the fundamentals of morality should be taught during these years; but he believed that instruction in these could be integrated into the teaching of the three major studies. Arithmetic, history, geography and reading and writ-

ing—all at a rudimentary level—were to be the only academic studies and skills made available to the majority of
students, that is to say, the impoverished students without
exceptional talent. After finishing their elementary schooling, the females of these students were expected to learn
the household arts from their mothers. The males were
expected to take up manual vocations—farming from
their fathers or crafts or seamanship through the apprenticeship system. By the close of their vocational training,
they would have had, Jefferson presumed, opportunity to
strengthen their faculties to a large extent; and, with the
aid of newspapers and community discussions, they would
be able to inform themselves of public events and issues.

The wealthy students and the gifted poor students—
the latter receiving public financial support—would pro-
ceed to secondary schooling[7] in which a mixture of liberal
and utilitarian studies was to be taught: Latin and Greek
and the modern European languages, English grammar,
geography, advanced arithmetic and plain geometry, surveying, and navigation. The classic languages were held to
be valuable as memory exercisers, sources of models of literary style, funds of moral wisdom, and tools for scientific
and scholarly research. The modern European languages
were seen as especially pertinent to the nation's diplomatic
needs and Virginia's international commerce. English
grammar was viewed as necessary for effective speech and
writing. Geography was regarded as helpful for enlarging
the students' understanding of the earth's physical aspects.
Advanced arithmetic and plain geometry were thought to
be especially useful for developing the rational faculty,
applicable to practical affairs, and preparatory for the
study of other branches of mathematics. Surveying was

considered important to Virginia's vast agricultural area
and the nation's frontier lands; and navigation was looked
upon as valuable to the state's maritime activities. Upon
completion of these secondary studies, Jefferson presumed, students would have considerably improved their
judgmental and auxiliary powers. The wealthy and the
extraordinarily gifted poor students were expected to seek
a university education. And the students who did not continue their education were to begin learning vocations requiring comparatively advanced language and mathematical abilities, such as commerce, navigation, and surveying.
Jefferson did not think that any of Virginia's female students would try to undertake this secondary schooling. He
did recognize that the wealthy female students would be
interested in schooling beyond the elementary level, but
he assumed that they would want nothing more than tu-
toring in a young lady's finishing education, which
involved belles-lettres, music, drawing, and one or two
modern languages. Apparently, he believed that even the
talented impoverished female students would seek to
acquire nothing more than the domestic arts.

The courses of study that Jefferson advised for the
University of Virginia, which included those called for in
his bill for reorganizing William and Mary, were extensive and diverse.[8] In addition to ancient and modern languages and advanced mathematics, there were courses in
physics, chemistry, mineralogy, biology, medicine, architecture, political philosophy, economics, geography, lin-
guistics, ethics, rhetoric, belles-lettres, and the fine arts.
Although Jefferson recommended that the courses in
mathematics and natural science be taught in their applied as well as their pure aspects, he thought that the

university's students, in order to be further cognizant of technology, should have the opportunity to receive training in the manual arts from master craftsmen. Recognizing that interests and abilities differ among individuals, he did not demand that there be just one course of study for the students but stated that students at the University of Virginia should be permitted to choose their own courses of study. (Jefferson may first have learned of the elective system of study when he was in Paris, where there was some advocacy of it.) Despite his allowance for electives in academic and technical studies, he argued that the university's students should be required to take military training, which was intended to furnish them with physical exercise as well as expertise as military officers. As far as one knows, Jefferson did not regard extra-curricular activities, such as choirs and drama groups, as appropriate to university education. So, with respect to its curriculum, the University of Virginia was planned to enable its students to acquire excellence in many of the fields of reason, morals, and aesthetics and, at the same time, to give its students special preparation for public leadership in Virginia and for numerous professions of value to the state.

Jefferson, however, advocated studies other than those to be offered by the schools and the University of Virginia. With reference to human knowledge, it has already been maintained, Jefferson's philosophical principles imply that it is possible to have historical progress in the different disciplines. This progress is possible, to an indefinite extent, insofar as man's judgmental faculties improve; and they can improve inasmuch as man accumulates knowledge, learns from his past mistakes, and experiences new circumstances. As a matter of fact, Jefferson claimed that there had been much progress in the disciplines from ancient times up to his own and that improvements were continually being made. For prima facie evidence, he pointed to what he regarded as man's enhanced moral sensitivity and to the advancements of modern science; and he referred to the continuing accomplishments in science and scholarship at the turn of the nineteenth century.[9] Because Jefferson viewed science and scholarship as two of the great potential benefactors of modern man, he stressed their importance for Virginia. And, because he saw the current advancements in science and scholarship as possible ways for enlarging the opportunities for happiness in the state, he emphasized the need for research and continuing education studies. He considered research as a means by which the state's scientists and scholars might keep informed of present work in their respective fields and make contributions of their own. And he believed continuing education especially to be the means for informing laymen of the pertinent applications of the new findings in science. Because Jefferson thought that the school and university institutions in Virginia should have the primary function of teaching what was well established, he perceived that other agencies were required in the state to foster research and continuing education in technology. His original proposal for a research facility for Virginia was his bill for a public library. Years later, he conceived his notion for a national philosophical academy, which was intended to encourage research for the nation as a whole. One of his proposals for an institution for continuing technological education was his project for the county agricultural societies. Another related to community libraries for the general public. Although he never devised a plan for the libraries, he did recommend that, if they were instituted in Virginia, they should supply books in mechanics and agriculture as well as other fields.

In planning a system of public education for Virginia, Jefferson entertained the question of how the system should be administrated. To answer it, he followed his theoretical proposal for decentralized educational administration; however, he was also guided by some broader considerations that he gave to the administrative structure of Virginia's government. In formulating a general scheme of governmental administration for Virginia, Jefferson followed his principle of decentralized government; and in considering specific types of regional and local governments for the state, he recurred partly to a present institution and partly to innovation. He thought that the division of the state into counties should be retained to provide regional governments, and he recommended that each county be divided into wards to institute local governments. Originally, as in the general education bill of 1779, he spoke of the county subdivisions as "hundreds"; but later, as in the general education bill of 1817, he referred to them as "wards." At any rate, this scheme of decentralized governmental administration greatly directed his thinking on how the public education that he was devising for Virginia should be administered.

Jefferson envisioned the ward in Virginia as a face-to-face political community.[10] Suggesting that it be about 6 miles square in area, he assumed that it would be small enough to permit an assembly of citizens to discuss important local issues and elect ward officials. But he also held that, in general, it would be sufficiently populous and

wealthy to take care of most of the problems of an immediate local concern. Although he recognized that his proposed elementary schools would be of significance to Virginia as a whole, he viewed them as being of direct
interest to the wards, because each ward would probably
have a child population large enough to require an elementary school. Consequently he advocated that an elementary school be situated in every ward, that it be locally
supported (by tax or some other means), and that a ward
official look after the maintenance of the school building.
Because Jefferson knew that the elementary schools would
ultimately be important to Virginia as a whole, he did not
think that their supervision should necessarily be reserved
exclusively for the individual wards. And, presuming that
many wards would not have persons qualified to oversee
the work of their schools, he decided, in the general education bill of 1817, that the work of the elementary
schools of each county should be supervised by resident
officers appointed by the county's superior court. Among
other duties, these supervisors would evaluate the quality
of instruction in the schools and select the promising poor
students to attend the secondary schools at public expense.
Jefferson did not think each county in Virginia had
enough secondary school students to fill a school. So, instead of being of primary interest to any one county, the
secondary school, Jefferson felt, would be important to a
cluster of counties that it might serve.[11] He recommended,
therefore, that a secondary school be located in a district
consisting of several adjacent counties and supported by
state monies. In accordance with the general education
bill of 1817, resident supervisors for each secondary district would be appointed by the state's Board of Public

Instruction and given general control of the district school, including the authority to select poor students to obtain a university education at public expense. The University of Virginia, of course, was regarded by Jefferson as a state institution. According to the education fund commission's report of 1818, the supervision and general control of the university was to be placed in the hands of the Board of Visitors, which was to be appointed by the state's executive or some other official person or persons whom the legislature should deem suitable for the purpose. The daily operations of the institution were to be overseen by the rector, who was to be elected by the visitors from one of their number. And the financial support of the university was to come largely from the state's education fund.[12]

In formulating his plans for public education in Virginia, Jefferson was compelled to entertain three questions concerning freedom. The first was how to preserve the students' religious freedom. On the one hand, Jefferson's political theory implied that the public educational institutions of a republic ought not to provide any religious doctrine; and the numerous religious groups of Virginia were equally insistent that public schools should not impart any teaching contrary to their respective creeds. On the other hand, Jefferson believed that it would be unfeasible to try to purge all possible religious observances and subject matters from the state's public schools and university. Therefore, he decided (as reflected by the general education bill of 1817) that all that was needed was to forbid the obvious possible threats to any religious group's doctrine: no ecclesiastical official should be appointed as public education supervisor; no religious reading, instruction, or exercise ought to be prescribed or practiced in the public educational institutions that would be inconsistent with the tenets of any religious sect or denomination; and there should be no professor of divinity at the University of Virginia.[13] Although these rules were rather restrictive, they made possible some religious observances and some study of religious subject matters. Holidays commonly shared by Virginia's various religious groups could be observed by the schools and the university. In the university, students of Greek and Hebrew could investigate, for scholarly purposes, Biblical texts; and students of philosophy could examine philosophical problems involved in the concept of God.[14]

The second question concerned the limits of academic freedom. Although Jefferson extolled the pursuit of truth and the freedom of expression as natural rights, he regarded the public schools and university in Virginia as institutions of Virginia's society and maintained that they be limited as such. Thus, far from granting autonomy to the University of Virginia, he stipulated that the state legislature might enact laws governing the rector and the Board of Visitors and, more broadly, that the university "should, in all things, and at all times, be subject to the control of the Legislature." [15] When, as rector, Jefferson gave consideration to establishing the university's professorship of law, he argued that the law curriculum must be favorable to Virginia's republican institutions; in fact, he even prescribed the text to be employed by the professor of law.[16]

The third question was how much control over Virginia's public education ought to be allowed the citizenry. Even though Jefferson felt that public education should exist in any republic only with a majority approval from the body of citizens, he was never inclined toward the position that ordinary citizens should directly regulate the substance and operations of public education—just as he never leaned toward the position that ordinary citizens ought to be public leaders. At the same time, he thought that the public had some rights in the control of public education, namely, the right to regulate the fiscal support of public education and to assure that education served the public welfare. To increase the possibility that the supervisors of the programs and operations of the state's schools and university would be suitably qualified, he specified that these officials be appointed by other officials rather than elected by the public. To provide the public with some regulation of public education finance, he made the wards directly responsible for the support of the elementary schools and put the support of the secondary schools and the university under the ultimate control of the state legislature. And, to help make certain that the University of Virginia would serve the public, he emphatically stated that it must be under the control of the legislature.

It has to be acknowledged that Jefferson's practical educational proposals were not without flaws. For instance, one doubts that the brief elementary schooling, which he recommended for the mass of students, would have been adequate to give Virginia an enlightened citizenry. One suspects that his rules for protecting the religious freedom of students were not sufficient to guard the freedom of conscience of the atheist student. One questions, in view of the current standard that gives professors the freedom to choose their textbooks, that Jefferson was right when he prescribed the textbooks to be used by the University of

Virginia's law professor. And one notices that he had very little to say about educational method. Why Jefferson's practical educational proposals involved these and other faults can be explained, to a significant degree, by several major points. (a) In conceiving the practical proposals, he followed his theoretical ones; and on occasion he was influenced by the latter where they were weak. For example, Jefferson's theoretical ideas included a sketchy consideration of educational method, and he was not prompted to consider the topic seriously in his practical educational proposals. (b) Because he strongly desired to see his plans for public education enacted into law, he applied his theoretical educational ideas, at times, to accommodate Virginia's circumstances. Therefore he advocated a meager elementary schooling because he did not think that Virginia could pay for a better one. And he wrote his rules governing the religious freedom of students with an eye to gaining the approval of the state's various religious groups. (c) Because he was immediately embroiled in the defense of Virginia's republican institutions, he ignored, from time to time, his political theory in defense of these institutions and resorted to expediency. His selecting the law textbooks may be regarded as a case of expediency. Since Jefferson wanted to insure that the future guardians of Virginia's legal institutions and practices would be imbued with a democratic view of law, he wanted to guarantee personally that the state's law students would study the textbooks that he thought democratic in orientation.

· NOTES ·

1. To Peter Carr (September 7, 1814), in A. A. Lipscomb and A. E. Bergh (eds.), *The Writings of Thomas Jefferson,* "Memorial Edition," 20 vols. (Washington, D.C.: Thomas Jefferson Memorial Association, 1903–1904), XIV, 213. Italics added.

2. To Philip Mazzei (November 1785), in Julian P. Boyd *et al.* (eds.), *The Papers of Thomas Jefferson,* 17 vols. published, 50 vols. projected (Princeton, N.J.: Princeton University Press, 1950 et seq.), IX, 68.

3. Cf. letter to Robert Skipwith (August 3, 1771), in Boyd, *op. cit.,* IX, 68. To Martha Jefferson (March 28, 1787), in Boyd, *op. cit.,* XI, 251. To Peter Carr (August 10, 1787), in Boyd, *op. cit.,* XII, 14–18. To Ralph Izard (July 17, 1788), in Boyd, *op. cit.,* XIII, 372–373. Also, see *supra,* pp. 53–54.

4. To Joel Barlow (February 24, 1806), in P. L. Ford (ed.), *The Works of Thomas Jefferson,* "Federal Edition," 12 vols. (New York: Putnam, 1904–1905), X, 232–233.

5. To Peter Carr (September 7, 1814), in Ford, *op. cit.,* X, 213.

6. Cf. "A Bill for Establishing a System of Public Education," in Roy J. Honeywell, *The Educational Work of Thomas Jefferson* (Cambridge, Mass.: Harvard University Press, 1931), p. 234.

7. Cf. *ibid.,* p. 237 f.

8. "Report of the Commissioners Appointed to Fix the Site of the University of Virginia, &c.," in Honeywell, *op. cit.,* pp. 252–257.

9. *Ibid.,* p. 251.

10. To Samuel Kercheval (July 12, 1816), in Ford, *op. cit.,* XII, 8–9.

11. "A Bill for Establishing a System of Public Education," in Honeywell, *op. cit.,* pp. 236–237.

12. "Report of the Commissioners Appointed to Fix the Site of the University of Virginia, &c.," in Honeywell, *op. cit.*, pp. 257–260.

13. "A Bill for Establishing a System of Public Education," in Honeywell, *op. cit.*, pp. 233, 235.

14. "Report of the Commissioners Appointed to Fix the Site of the University of Virginia, &c.," in Honeywell, *op. cit.*, p. 256.

15. *Ibid.*, p. 258.

16. "An Exact Transcript of the Minutes of the Board of Visitors of the University of Virginia, during the Rectorship of Thomas Jefferson," in Lipscomb and Bergh, *op. cit.*, XIX, 460–461.

·VI·
Contributions to Western Education

Thomas Jefferson's educational proposals, it has been argued, are grounded upon his philosophical ideas; and by virtue of this philosophical basis, they involve certain contributions to Western education. Although these contributions are not the only ones included in the proposals, they deserve special attention. Until this time, scholars concerned with Jefferson's educational thought have tended to ignore them.

Jefferson's theoretical educational proposals, one will remember, provide a general statement on education in republican, or democratic, society. Without question, the statement was hardly the first of its kind to appear. The subject had been discussed by philosophers, including both opponents and supporters of democracy, as early as Plato and Aristotle and as late as Montesquieu and Rousseau. Furthermore, Jefferson's statement is unsatisfactory in some areas. It offers, for example, very little assistance in a consideration of which method or methods are suitable to education in a democracy. Nevertheless, Jefferson's formulation of education in democracy must be regarded as important. Since his day, democratic institutions have gradually spread among Western societies; and, as a result, many educators have been confronted with the problem of the place of education in a democracy. Consequently, Jefferson's view of education in democracy, by concerning an educational problem that has been relevant to Western society during the past 150 years or so, has remained pertinent to Western educational thought long after Jefferson's time. In addition, his view has positively influenced some notable educators—to name a current example, James B. Conant, the former president of Harvard University, who has made many studies of American public schools.[1]

There is still another reason for the importance of Jefferson's statement of education in democratic society. From ancient times to the present, the place of education in democracy has undergone a variety of philosophical inquiries. But, despite the variety, Jefferson's investigation of the problem has been rather distinct. By involving a metaphysical realism, which allows that some existing things are what they are independently of human beings, his investigation differs from inquiries that have followed the principles of pragmatism. The pragmatists, as exemplified by John Dewey, the twentieth-century American philosopher and educator, have usually held that what exists is determined to some extent by human experience. Because of its comprehension of a strict empiricism and materialism, Jefferson's inquiry varies notably from the rationalist investigations (which presuppose that knowledge of existence may be independent of sense experience) and from those undertaken by Thomists, who maintain that some existing things, such as God and man's soul, are spiritual and not material. And, inasmuch as Jefferson's position embraces a moral sense theory, it departs from the Aristotelian position, which rejects the notion of a special moral faculty. Jefferson's investigation does resemble, in striking ways, the inquiries that were undertaken by a few of his contemporaries, for example, the Pennsylvania physician Benjamin Rush; but Jefferson differs from his contemporaries on several notable points, for instance, in the areas of psychology and ethics. Thus, Rush held that the conscience is seated in the understanding and that the moral faculty is located in the will; whereas Jefferson did not distinguish between the conscience and the moral faculty and did not maintain that there is a special faculty for the will. In brief, Jefferson's theoretical view on education in a democracy is grounded on a philosophical position that is an alternative to the sorts of positions taken by the other investigators of the problem. His view, as a consequence, has enriched Western educational thought. Because it rests on a fairly distinct philosophical basis, it is frequently different from the theoretical views found in the other investigations of education's place in democratic society. And, even where it is similar to them, it is justified by principles often varying from those supporting the other views.

Whereas Jefferson's theoretical proposals have provided a general formulation of education's role in democratic society, the practical proposals have furnished programs and plans for education in a particular democracy. These programs and plans, it is ordinarily acknowledged, are open to numerous criticisms. For instance, the formal schooling allowed by them for the mass of students appears to have been too meager to have furnished Virginia with an enlightened citizenry. But in spite of the weaknesses of the proposals, there is ground for deeming them significant.

One point is that they involve some originality. Although Jefferson was by no means the first, even in the modern era of Western society, to express a theoretical view on the topic of education in democracy, he was certainly among the early few in the modern period to advance educational programs and plans of an explicit democratic nature for a particular society. To be sure, there were schemes devised and enacted, in both Europe and the American colonies, for mass education prior to Jefferson's general education bill of 1779; but virtually all of them were formulated according to principles favoring aristocratic, ecclesiastical, or burgher social orders. Moreover, before the American Revolution, which included, perhaps, the first major effort in modern Western society to establish a democratic social order, modern advocates of democracy rarely had an occasion to conceive concrete measures for democratic education. The fact that Jefferson was among the early few to present practical proposals, especially in the general education bill of 1779, means that his may be regarded as a likely beginning of the many concrete measures for democratic education that have been integral to Western education in the modern era. Another point is that Jefferson's programs and plans for education in Virginia and the nation have exercised a fair amount of influence. When Jefferson was alive, the programs and plans were seriously received and discussed by numerous of his fellow Americans, including members of the American Philosophical Society, and were also favorably studied by some Europeans keenly interested in education, for example, Du Pont de Nemours. After Jefferson's death, the programs and plans were accepted, mainly in the American South, as guides for establishing public education. Although these proposals exerted most of their immediate influence in the South, they have had an indirect and lasting influence throughout the nation. The existence of the public schools, their concern with fostering democracy, their organization on a state-wide basis, and their control by agencies responsible to the public—these features of education in America today have their origins, at least in part, in Jefferson's proposals for education in Virginia.

A third point is less obvious. As already indicated, the programs and plans are explicable and justifiable, at a general level, by Jefferson's theoretical educational proposals and, ultimately, by his philosophical principles. Because the programs and plans do rest on a philosophical foundation, they asume a definite value when compared to the great majority of practical proposals on democratic education that have been presented since Jefferson's day. Although the bulk of these later proposals have been accompanied by such words as "liberty," "equality," and "citizenship," it is not at all apparent that the great proportion of them have been conceived with reference to any philosophical principles. These proposals recommend, for instance, that students be taught to value liberty and equality and be trained to perform the duties of democratic citizenship; but they fail to specify the meaning of liberty and equality and explicate the duties of democratic citizenship. They have been framed largely by nothing more than empty rhetoric. At any rate, they have frequently lacked fundamental clarity and justification.[2] Jefferson's programs and plans, therefore, stand as a reminder that the vast majority of the proposals that have been rendered to solve the practical problems of democratic education in Western society could have been better clarified and justified if they had been given a philosophical orientation. Also, the programs and plans serve to remind current Western philosophers of education, some of whom have shown doubts about the value of philosophy for providing solutions to concrete educational problems, that philosophical ideas have been useful in conceiving practical measures relating to democratic education at least.

Although it is not readily evident that Jefferson's theoretical educational proposals say anything about science that is especially notable in Western education, he has made contributions in the area of science education. Comments on science education in the proposals are scanty: Jefferson does little more than name and briefly define various scientific disciplines, discuss the importance of science education in democracy, and suggest (but not examine) a science curriculum for schools in a democratic society. Upon a scrutiny of their philosophical foundation, however, Jefferson's theoretical proposals can be seen to be significant insofar as they imply the value of science to humanity. With reference to Jefferson's philosophical principles, science is valuable to men to the degree that it can promote their happiness; and the teaching of the discipline bears human value only when its aim is man's happiness. On the surface, this statement has nothing about it that was novel during Jefferson's day. Similar statements about the importance of science had been made by a number of other educational thinkers at the time and had been foreshadowed by the writings of Francis Bacon among others. Nevertheless, Jefferson's view of the value of science education brought into focus an issue that had received little consideration before and during Jefferson's day and that has steadily gained in moment since then. The issue is the different usages to which various sorts of society might put science education. Happiness, it must be recalled, can be achieved only in a society and is most likely to be attained in a democracy. Science, then, in order to be employed for the happiness of men, must operate within a society; and, seemingly, it is most likely to be put to this end within a democracy. So, science education is most likely to be made to help achieve man's proper end in a democratic society. It follows, for Jefferson, that science education is likely to be used to increase human misery when it is established in tyrannical societies.[3] Prior to and during the eighteenth century, the potential human benefits of science education were frequently discussed; but the various usages to which different types of society might put science education were rarely examined. Subsequently, the increasing use of technology for the achievement of political aims—including social, military, and economic ones—has made the issue a subject of expanded and heightened interest.

Jefferson's practical proposals on science education are important mainly because they constitute a historical landmark, but they do not derive this importance from his philosophical ideas. Concrete measures for modern science education were not uncommon when Jefferson lived; indeed, study of the new science had been acquiring an acceptance at various European universities at least since the beginning of the eighteenth century. Nevertheless, his recommendations for the teaching of science in Virginia may be regarded as one of the notable marks in the development of modern science education in Western society. Jefferson's proposals preceded by many decades the general acceptance of serious science programs in higher educational institutions: in the second half of the nineteenth century, it must be remembered, Herbert Spencer, in England, and Charles Eliot, in America, found it necessary to plead the cause of science education. Moreover, unlike many science programs presented by other educators in the eighteenth century and the early part of the nineteenth, Jefferson's proposals accorded a large place to the study of science.

A further contribution by Jefferson to Western education may be found in his educational proposals as they relate to meritocracy, the idea that positions in society should be allocated to persons according to their respective merits. Throughout Western history various criteria have been utilized to determine the actual distribution of positions in society. Family, wealth, military prowess, popularity, race, and religion are some of the commonly known ones. However, a number of Western social critics, ranging from Plato through Karl Marx and John Dewey, have argued, in general, that there is only one satisfactory criterion, merit. That is, they have contended that citizens should occupy only those positions for which they have the necessary abilities. In Western educational thought, accordingly, there has been a fairly strong theoretical interest in how education might be employed to prepare the members of society for positions appropriate to their abilities. Jefferson's theoretical view of education for a social order based on merit was among the first to relate to democracy. (Practically all predecessors to his view and most of its contemporaries centered on aristocratic, ecclesiastical, and oligarchical social organizations.) In keeping with Jefferson's political thought, the individual members of a democracy should hold only those positions within the society that are commensurate with their respective abilities. The citizens with extraordinarily strong judgmental powers ought to provide the society with public and private leadership; and the citizens with weaker faculties of judgment should furnish the society with common laborers, skilled workers, clerks, etc.

Jefferson's conception of education for a merit-based social order, unlike theories posed by some other educational thinkers, is rather profound. Jefferson set the conception within the framework of his philosophical ideas. And, being led by them, he discussed in basic terms many major issues connected with education for a social order based on merit, for instance: to what extent are abilities determined by natural endowment and to what extent by training? Should all competences be developed, or only those which are morally approbative? Can the abilities of a present generation of students be developed beyond those of the past generation, or is there no historical progress in human abilities?

Although Jefferson's philosophical principles help make his theoretical educational proposals significant to Western education as they pertain to a merit system, they hold no special importance for his practical educational proposals in this respect. It must be mentioned, nonetheless, that the practical proposals have been somewhat contributive to a merit system of education in Western society. Mainly, they contain measures that along with similar ones offered by other educators, were forerunners of systems widely employed today to ensure the education of students according to their abilities. The most notable of these are the recommendations for public financial support of a general system of education, special financial aid for promising indigent students, and different levels of formal education for students with various levels of ability.

Finally, Jefferson's educational proposals have to be considered as they concern the role of religion in public education. Jefferson contended that the legitimate aim of the government of any state is to protect the natural rights of the state's citizens, and he held that the freedom of the mind is a natural right. Thus, he argued that no public educational institution should impose upon its students religious teachings or practices contrary to their individual beliefs. By taking this position, Jefferson became one of the initiators of the movement in modern Western educational thought toward a removal of religious instruction and practice from public education. During his time the position was also assumed by the atheistic French philosophers, deistic theologians, and the leaders of a few Protestant groups, among others; however, it was rejected then by the bulk of educational theorists, who regarded religious teaching and practice as the basis of moral training, public and private. At present, the position is commonly, but by no means universally, accepted.

Jefferson, it has been explained, maintained that

public moral training can feasibly be undergone without reliance upon religious indoctrination or practice; he proposed that it can be acquired from the reading of history and morally sound literature, from pedagogical advice and admonishment, and from association with virtuous people. And he founded this recommendation upon his moral sense theory of ethics, which attributes a divine origin to morality. Because of its being grounded on this theory, the recommendation occupies a special place in Western educational thought. By excluding the proposition that moral training requires a religious base, it disagrees with what seems to be a majority of the recommendations, by other educational theorists, which include the proposition that morality stems from God. And, by attributing to morality a divine source, it differs from many of the recommendations, by other educational theorists, which dismiss religious teaching and practice from public moral training. Apparently, the recommendation should be of interest to present-day educators who shun orthodox ecclesiastical approaches to public moral training but who do not find atheistic and agnostic orientations acceptable.

As previously intimated, there appears to be a disparity between Jefferson's philosophical principles and his practical proposals concerning the place of religion in public education. For instance, the general education bill of 1817 asserted that it would be permissible to observe, in the public schools proposed for Virginia, religious practices that were commonly shared by all religious groups in the state. And it was pointed out that this measure seems to be inconsistent with the atheist student's freedom of mind. Although this disparity indicates that Jefferson's practical proposals on religion's role in public education present difficulties, one should not fail to see that they have a definite importance. Succinctly, they are some of the first measures in modern Western history to specify a virtually secular system of public education for a given society. Although they did make permissible some religious instruction and practice in Virginia's public education, they did not require any; and they explicitly attributed only political and other secular purposes to such education. One is hard put to find in modern Western history concrete schemes for a virtually secular public education that antedate the general education bill of 1779. Accordingly, Jefferson's practical educational proposals may be taken as an original of the innumerable plans for secular public education that have been presented in Western society since his time.

· NOTES ·

1. See James B. Conant, *Education and Liberty* (New York: Random House, 1953), pp. vii–xii.
2. Cf. Robert D. Heslep, "Political Theory and Education's Role in the United States," *Educational Theory*, XIV (July 1964), 174–181.
3. Cf. letter to John Adams (January 21, 1812), in L. J. Cappon (ed.), *The Adams-Jefferson Letters*, 2 vols. (Chapel Hill: The University of North Carolina Press, 1959), II, 291.

Bibliography

ORIGINAL SOURCES
No single collection of Jefferson's writings is entirely satis-
factory; one must select from among various publications with
regard to their strengths and weaknesses. The following list
should prove adequate for the student interested in Jefferson's
philosophical and educational views.

The Papers of Thomas Jefferson, Julian P. Boyd et al. (eds.),
17 vols. published, 50 vols. projected. Princeton, N.J.:
Princeton University Press, 1950 et seq. This is one of
the best editions of Jefferson's works, providing, in chronological order, copies of letters, receipts, official papers, and
other documents not found in any other collection; the
editing is superb, and there are two convenient index volumes. The present volumes do not go beyond Jefferson's
papers written during Washington's administration, nor do
they include his *Notes on the State of Virginia.*

The Works of Thomas Jefferson, "Federal Edition," P. L.
Ford (ed.), 12 vols. New York: Putnam, 1904–1905.
Arranged chronologically, this collection covers the period

of Jefferson's extant writing, although omitting several letters and papers of philosophical and educational value. (Indexed)

The Writings of Thomas Jefferson, "Memorial Edition," A. A. Lipscomb and A. E. Bergh (eds.), 20 vols. Washington, D.C.: Thomas Jefferson Memorial Association, 1903–1904. This edition covers, in chronological order, the whole time span of Jefferson's extant writing; it contains philosophically and educationally significant letters found in neither the Boyd nor Ford volumes. Jefferson's spelling and punctuation have been modernized in numerous instances. (Indexed)

The Commonplace Book of Thomas Jefferson: A Repertory of His Ideas on Government, with an Introduction and notes by Gilbert Chinard. Baltimore: The Johns Hopkins University Press, 1926. Although not precisely a repertory of Jefferson's ideas on government, this volume does consist of quotations and paraphrases from political works read by Jefferson mostly prior to the American Revolution. This volume is indispensable for understanding what shaped Jefferson's political thought.

The Literary Bible of Thomas Jefferson: His Commonplace Book of Philosophers and Poets, with an Introduction by Gilbert Chinard. Baltimore: The Johns Hopkins University Press, 1928. Containing quotations from philosophical and literary works read by Jefferson chiefly during his student years, this volume is quite helpful with the origins of his thinking on ethics.

Crusade Against Ignorance: Thomas Jefferson on Education, with an Introduction by Gordon C. Lee. New York: Bureau of Publications of Teachers College, Columbia University, 1962. This is a convenient anthology of Jefferson's philosophical and educational writings, although several important writings are omitted.

SECONDARY SOURCES
Although there is no abundance of interpretations of Jefferson's philosophical and educational thought, there are several which might prove more useful to the student than others.

Brown, Stuart G. *Thomas Jefferson.* New York: Washington Square Press, 1963. A compact scholarly biography of Thomas Jefferson, this work offers an incisive discussion of Jefferson's philosophical views on nature, morals, and politics, although the treatment of his educational ideas is somewhat short.

Honeywell, Roy J. *The Educational Work of Thomas Jefferson.* Cambridge, Mass.: Harvard University Press, 1931. This volume ignores Jefferson's philosophical ideas and theoretical educational proposals, but furnishes a first-rate examination of his practical educational proposals. It includes appendices of Jefferson's major programs and plans of education.

Koch, Adrienne. *The Philosophy of Thomas Jefferson.* New York: Columbia University Press, 1943. This volume examines closely the origins of Jefferson's philosophical thought and includes a discussion of his philosophical principles, but the treatment of his educational views is superficial.

BACKGROUND MATERIAL
There are several volumes especially helpful for understanding the historical context in which Jefferson developed his philosophical and educational ideas.

Bruce, Philip A. *Institutional History of Virginia in the Seventeenth Century,* 2 vols. New York: Putnam, 1910. Details of the political, social, and cultural institutions of seventeenth-century Virginia are examined.

Malone, Dumas. *Jefferson the Virginian,* Vol. I of *Jefferson and His Time,* 3 vols. published, 4 vols. projected. Boston: Little, Brown, 1948. This first volume of an exhaustive but as yet unfinished biographical study offers a detailed account of Jefferson's ancestry, childhood, youth, and early manhood.

————. *Jefferson and the Rights of Man,* Vol. II of *Jefferson and His Time,* 3 vols. published, 4 vols. projected. Boston: Little, Brown, 1951. This volume of Professor Malone's prodigious undertaking is especially informative on Jefferson's stay in France and other countries of Europe.

Morton, Richard L. *Colonial Virginia,* 2 vols. Chapel Hill: The University of North Carolina Press, 1960. These volumes are a well-documented chronological account of colonial Virginia.

Wertenbaker, Thomas J. *The Planters of Colonial Virginia.* Princeton, N.J.: Princeton University Press, 1922. This book is a judicious analysis of the plantation system of colonial Virginia.

Index